MW00627466

LET'S TALK

DOM SKINNER

Words by Dom

LET'S TALK

CHANGING THE NARRATIVE AND SEEING MY MOTHER AS HUMAN

Dom Skinner

© Copyright 2021 by Dom Skinner – All rights reserved.

It is not legal to reproduce, duplicate, or transmit any part of this document in either electronic means or printed format. Recording of this publication is strictly prohibited.

FIRST EDITION

DESIGNED BY JESSICA ALEXANDRA CANCINO

ISBN: 978-0-578-30981-1

Before I formed you in the
womb I knew you, before
you were born I sat you
apart

JEREMIAH 1:5

Dom Skinner

Dedication

With a heart full of gratitude, I give thanks and praise to God for creating my path. This book is dedicated to every one of my parents, Phyllis Skinner, Keith "Checko" Jones, Timothy "Timmy" Skinner, Steve Douglas, Vaughn Perry, and Krislyn "Krissi" Perry. I am all that I am because of you. Each of you has added pieces to my puzzle.

To the woman responsible for bringing me into this world, my mother, Phyllis, thank you for always being on the ride with me, no matter how bumpy it may get. There aren't enough words to express how grateful I am to say, 'I am my mother's daughter.' Thank you for showing me what strength and resilience look like through your countless sacrifices for my sisters and me. You have given us your best. Now, you get to give your best to YOU because you are worthy of it.

To my father, Checko, thank you for exemplifying the importance of calm and serenity. As a man of few words, I feel honored every time I learn something new from you. Thank you for sharing your love with me.

To my godfather, Steve, thank you for keeping your promises. Thank you for making sure I always had the best, from traveling abroad, to participating in sports and activities, to books for school, and the list goes on. I'll never take for granted the support you've added to my journey.

Additionally, I will never get tired of saying 'Thank you for adopting me into your world' to my faithful adopted parents, Vaughn and Krissi Perry. I am forever grateful for your unwavering dedication to love me through my pain, doubt, and internal chaos. Thank you for seeing me as whole when I was experiencing brokenness.

Finally, I would like to pour out a heavenly thank you to Timmy for gifting me a very cool name. May your soul rest in peace.

Like my mother, Phyllis would say, "God always gives us what we need to survive." God indeed poured down blessings over my life when He assigned each of you to be my parent. Thank you for accepting me as your assignment. Because of what each of you has given me, I get to be dynamic in my complexities.

I love you all!

Your daughter,
Dominique
"Dom"

TABLE OF CONTENTS

Dom Skinner

Chapter One:

Going Against the Grain

Dom Skinner

As the story goes, on December 2, 1989, in Washington, DC, Phyllis Skinner, barely 8 months pregnant, went to the hospital for a routine prenatal appointment. During this appointment, the nurse informed her that she'd started dilating and needed to be prepared for delivery. Phyllis, in her demanding manner, reassured the nurse that she was okay. She also reminded the nurse that she was not a first-time mother. She'd know if she was in labor, plus it was too early for her child to be delivered. The nurse allowed her to go on with her story while moving her to a labor and delivery room.

After the nurse dismissed Phyllis saying, "the doctor will be in here soon," Phyllis asked for a bible.

Before she knew it, Phyllis felt pressure from her belly. The pressure was the reassurance that she was, in fact, in labor. As the pain started to fill her body, she called for the nurse. The stress and the pain were clear signs of the baby's urgent arrival. Phyllis prepared herself the best way she knew how. She scooted her body towards the top of the bed, going as far back as she could, then she grabbed the nearby bible and started to speak out loud to God.

Through her prayer, Phyllis took deep breaths, inhaling deeply and exhaling slowly. Knowing that it was time, she began to push while she gripped the bible and yelled her prayers throughout the room. Within minutes, Phyllis gave birth to her fourth and final child. Laying in a pool of blood and still connected through the umbilical cord, Phyllis and the baby laid at opposite ends of the bed, simply being without a witness.

After minutes, a nurse entered, and to her surprise, the baby had already made an entrance into the world. The nurse yelled out of the room, "She had the baby! Get the doctor!" before she rushed to make sure both Phyllis and her new baby weren't in any danger.

So many emotions and thoughts filled the room. When the doctor ran in, he immediately tended to the premature baby, as the nurse tended to Phyllis. Then the doctor placed the baby in Phyllis' arms, saying, "It's a girl. She weighs 5 pounds, 2 ounces. She's a healthy one."

This is how I entered the world; early, unexpected, and without a party of medical professionals or loved ones there to welcome me, just God, my mother, and me. God's plan for my grand entrance was orchestrated and influenced my name, Dominique Briana, not quite my last name. We'll get to that later.

My name was going to be Briana, after my mother's younger brother, Brian. However, the doctor helped to change Phyllis' mind when he finally placed me in her arms and jokingly said, "This one has a dominant spirit. She is strong and mighty. Dominique is more fitting for her first name."

My mother agreed, and just like that, I was Dominique. Then hours later, my mother's husband signed his name on my birth certificate as "father," making my last name Skinner. Because he was not my father, this was the seed that planted years of confusion and distrust.

Some things are not what they seem, and other things are exactly what they're supposed to be.

Chapter Two:
Plans Change

Dom Skinner

Before giving birth to me, Phyllis was separated from her husband for a little over 3 years. Yet, he signed his name on a birth certificate for a child that did not share his blood. So, how did we get here?

Phyllis had a crush on an older guy in her neighborhood named Timothy. But everyone called him Timmy. He was a few years older than she was, but at 14 years old, two years is a lot. This guy was four years her senior, and he was watching her as much as she was watching him. Before you start judging extremely hard, picture the times.

It's the late 1970's, in Washington, DC, and Phyllis was fly. She created her own style that always had people asking about her clothes. She was spunky in her appearance and demeanor. So, the streets nicknamed her Spunky. Phyllis was also slick at the mouth. She could fight, so she didn't discriminate on who she'd give words to, except her elders, of course. Her mother didn't allow disrespect.

So, this older fella, Timmy, was checking her out. I'm assuming that Phyllis was probably acting like an adult, especially since she has many younger siblings. Anyway, after a year or so of them flirting with each other, they made it official. And if you're wondering what it means to 'be official' in this story, just keep following along, and it'll become clear. I'm not entirely sure if their relationship was accepted by Phyllis' mother, Helen. Still, before there could be a permanent contesting, Phyllis became pregnant.

A few months after her 18th birthday, in January of 1980, she gave birth to her first daughter, Nekisha. Becoming a teenage mother was not in Phyllis' plans. She was dreaming of following the steps of her older cousins and attending college. Instead, she dropped out of high school and started working to provide for her child.

Phyllis was the oldest of her mother's six children. She saw herself as an assistant parent to help raise her younger sisters and brothers while her stepfather worked or just lived his life. Once Phyllis became a mother, her focus shifted to figuring out how to actually be a parent. She couldn't just say "I don't feel like it" whenever she wanted a break, like operating as just the oldest child. Phyllis was now the adult she pretended to be, and she vowed to always give her child better than what she had, no matter what it took.

The first task on her agenda was to get out of her parents' 4-bedroom house in the Woodland Terrace public housing projects. After a year of working and saving, she moved into a newly developed apartment complex in southeast Washington, DC. This apartment seemed like luxury compared to where she'd grown up. It was covered in a nice plush carpet, there was a washing machine in her unit, and it had a large balcony. For a 19-year-old woman with a child, it was grand. Eventually, Timmy moved in, and, as she would say, "they started playing house."

A few years later, Phyllis and Timmy were convinced that the best thing for their child was to make their family official by getting married. Against her better judgment, at age 21, Phyllis Dunn became Phyllis Skinner. She married her childhood crush with hopes of doing everything 'the right way.' Two years into their marriage, Phyllis was confident that she'd made a mistake. She wanted a partner in parenting and marriage. Yet, she felt like she was doing it alone, while her husband, much like her stepfather, was often out living his life.

Phyllis and her husband, Timmy, were essentially two kids trying to navigate life as a union and parents during the height of the crack epidemic in Washington, DC. While neither used the drug, the city was plagued with abuse, robberies, a corrupt justice system, and broken homes. The high demand for the drug left Washington, DC, and its people in dismay. Respectability became questionable throughout the entire city, and in the home,

8

Phyllis was attempting to create with her husband. Their home became a breeding ground for insecurity and abuse because of infidelity. She was fed up and wanted out of her marriage. When she gathered the courage to leave, Phyllis received more unexpected news. She was pregnant with their second child.

Now a mother of two daughters, Nekisha and Ashley, Phyllis was even more determined to make things work in her marriage. She was taught to figure it out. I believe "taught" was used often in the way she'd explain her upbringing. However, she wasn't given the tools or strategies on how to "figure it out." So, her understanding was to accept her circumstances and continue to do the duties of a mother and wife.

It was 1986, and the times were changing. Phyllis, AKA Spunky, wasn't good with the "accept your circumstances and be a good wife" part. She was over it. She said if she was going to do it by herself, she would be by herself. As a result, Phyllis officially separated from her husband with the hopes of being divorced within six months. Her plans were interrupted again, and that did not happen.

Because it's the only way you've seen it done. doesn't mean it's the "right way" or the only way to do it.

Upgraded To the Unexpected

Young, still fly, and almost a free woman, Phyllis was moving on. While minding her business at a bus stop, a man with a foreign accent approached her. He introduced himself as Checko. She couldn't understand a word he was saying, but she liked it, so she entertained it for a while. Then, she noticed him more in her apartment complex. Phyllis wasn't sure if she was seeing him because she was no longer with her husband or if he was making himself known to her. She kept her eyes on him and realized he was a mysterious person who was methodical in how he moved. Side note, my mother should have been a spy.

Anyway, this Jamaican man, Checko, finally asked her out. She accepted the invitation out of pure curiosity because she didn't think they had anything in common. Phyllis soon learned that Checko was everything she'd desired in a partner; a provider, protector, teacher, friend, and lover. There was one concern. He was a professional drug dealer. After a while, this didn't bother her because he was spoiling her and her two daughters. Phyllis was falling head over heels, and her husband was angry that he was losing any chance of getting her back, so he refused to grant her a divorce. But Phyllis didn't allow that to stop her joy.

Phyllis was riding high in a bubble of love that she was growing in with her new man. She was mesmerized by him. This man had the heart of a lion, yet he wasn't forceful or abrasive. He was calm and present. He wasn't like any man she'd ever met. He didn't raise his voice, and he didn't speak unless he had something to say. He wasn't slick or fast-talking. He listened and watched everything and everyone; he was aware of everything happening around him. Like I said, he was a professional drug dealer.

When he became sure that he could trust Phyllis, he taught her his language, culture, food, and lifestyle. He also revealed that his mother named him Keith. As their relationship grew, so did her financial security, which allowed her luxuries she'd never experienced. She no longer had to work, and the finest jewelry, clothes, furs, and cars were available at her request. She was living a dream, but her new lifestyle didn't come without precautions. She was now a target for anyone who wanted to harm him, so her movements and mentality shifted. Her new lover helped sharpen her wits which became necessary for survival.

At the height of this exciting chapter of her life, Phyllis became pregnant. She was expecting her third child with her Jamaican lover. Although there was excitement around this new baby, Phyllis was also experiencing shame that she was still legally married but was with a different man. Then, there was a switch. The honeymoon phase of their relationship started to dwindle and be replaced with insecurities, fear, and paranoia. The fear and paranoia were the side effects of operating a successful drug business. However, the insecurities embedded in their household were internal battles that neither settled before entering this relationship. When the insecurities started to creep in, the jealousy raged out. So, while this pregnancy was supposed to be a beautiful time of shared love, it turned into a time that brought out the worst in Phyllis and Checko. She became a prisoner to the life she created with the man she was madly in love with.

In September of 1988, Phyllis' life was drastically changing before her eyes. She gave birth to her third daughter, Sade', her only child to carry the Dunn's name. Checko was at the height of his drug career with more money and power. The lovely neighborhood that Phyllis moved to years ago became ridden with drug activity and violence. The paradise and oasis that she once had were no longer present. Women began to invite themselves into her relationship, and the insecurity wounds began to deepen.

Phyllis was now living on an emotional rollercoaster filled with arguments, love, fighting, and more love. She was torn between staying and leaving while knowing what was best for her and her children. Yet, Checko made it very clear that leaving with their child wasn't an option. Like many mothers, there was no way Phyllis was going without her child. There were moments when she'd leave, and he'd find her and force her to release their baby to him.

This man was cut from a different cloth. She'd never met a man who fought so hard for their child, and she truly believed that Checko would have killed her to get to his daughter. Despite their domestic abuse, Phyllis loved him beyond words. He was crazy for her and even crazier for his child. She admired his tenacity, although she hated the emotional instability within their relationship.

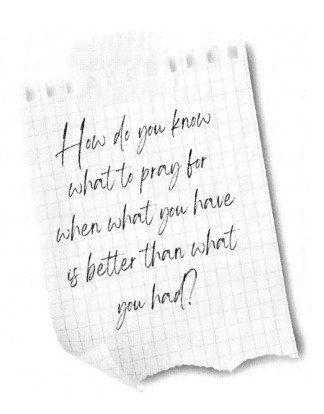

How do you know what to pray for when what you have is better than what you had?

Feeling Out of Control

Months after bringing home the newest member of her family, Phyllis received a call from Jamaica that created another shift in her life. Checko's mother, who usually called a few times a month to check in, called this time to inform Phyllis that she had a dream about fish. Phyllis was confused but assumed it meant something significant. This woman had used a calling card to call America to tell her about her dream. So, naturally, Phyllis asked Checko's mother the meaning of her dream.

The woman replied, "you're pregnant."

Phyllis almost laughed and wanted to call her crazy, but instead, she just denied it. There was no way she could be pregnant, and how would a woman in another country know this information? More importantly, Phyllis couldn't believe this news, even if she tried. There was no way she wanted to bring another baby into the chaos that she was praying to get out of. Phyllis was literally asking God for strength to cut ties with the man who had a magnetic pull on her heart.

She'd never loved someone as much as she loved him. She'd also never experienced someone who fought for her presence. To her, this had to be true love. Her relationship with Checko was very different from what she viewed in her parents' marriage. So, she assumed that she was experiencing heightened passion and euphoric love, to the point of senseless love. As a result, Phyllis often felt like she was going insane and couldn't think straight, so she was praying for peace and sanity.

A few days later, the prophecy that was spoken over her was confirmed. Phyllis was pregnant with her fourth child. Before she could fully settle her thoughts on what she was feeling, her prayer began to manifest in a series of unfortunate events.

A few days after her pregnancy was confirmed, Checko was arrested, detained, and scheduled for deportation back to

Jamaica. Soon after, there was a massive raid in their community. Many of the homes were searched and destroyed by the police department. Money and drugs were confiscated, people were killed, and many were arrested. Phyllis' house was among the homes affected by the raid, and she lost everything that kept her secured.

Phyllis was devastated and didn't know where to turn. She was aware that her new lifestyle with her Jamaican lover had isolated her from her friends and family. She didn't know how to return with nothing but shame, three daughters, and a few weeks pregnant with another child.

In her lowest moment, Phyllis went to her mother, Helen, for guidance, yet Helen didn't know how to support her. Phyllis left home with one child and was returning with three. Helen didn't have the space or resources, so she sent Phyllis to her mother, Celestia.

Phyllis' grandmother, Celestia, was a strong and loving woman but didn't believe in moping around or feeling sorry for herself. Instead, she taught her children and grandchildren the importance of prayer, keeping family together, and survival. After raising thirteen children, Grandma Celestia knew a thing or two about strength and resilience. So, when Phyllis came to her feeling broken and lost, she informed her that she wasn't the first woman to have a child out of her marriage and that she wouldn't be the last.

Grandma Celestia had a way of making everything seem like "a matter of fact." In this same tone, she reminded Phyllis that there were still comforts in being a married woman, then instructed her to give her unborn child to her husband. In other words, her grandmother told her to go back to her husband and rekindle their relationship to provide some stability for her unborn child.

Unaware of what else to do, Phyllis obeyed and went back to her husband, Timmy. Once they were settled into their renewed relationship, she revealed her pregnancy, leading him to believe that the unborn child was his seed. Yet, throughout her pregnancy, Timmy often asked if the child was from him.

Phyllis would respond, "This is my baby."

Her response was always enough to end the conversation. Until it wasn't. Eventually, the arguments and their history became too much. Phyllis decided that she wanted peace, which meant she had to abandon the advice she'd received from her grandmother. She took a chance on herself and left her husband again. This time she didn't have money saved up or an apartment with her name on it. But that didn't stop her from leaving. She packed up and took her three daughters to a shelter.

Every decision yields an outcome. Sometime, no matter your intentions, the outcome may not be in your favor.

Time to Rebuild

At 26 years old, Phyllis was a single mother of three children, pregnant, and living in a shelter. This was not how she expected her life to turn out. Just years ago, she'd made a vow to always give her child, now children, better than what her parents were able to provide. But her current situation was not living up to that promise. She'd gone from a teenage mother to a young wife, to the first lady of a successful drug operation, to a welfare candidate, all within nine years. Every one of her decisions up to that point was influenced by her love for a man.

Now, Phyllis was in a shelter, and the men weren't there to help pick up the pieces of the woman they'd broken. It was time for her to rebuild herself, and she decided that she would need strength from God to do it. She began to lean into her faith and fall back on the prayers that her grandmother had taught her. Phyllis declared that it would just be her and her children when God blessed her with a home. She was specific to add, "and no man." She wanted to make good on her vow, and she believed that a man could potentially be a distraction from being a good mother.

A few days after Phyllis entered the shelter, her youngest daughter, Sade', turned a year old. She refused to celebrate her child in a place where she felt hopeless. Instead, Phyllis had a small party at her aunt's house so that her girls could enjoy the day with their family. During the party, Phyllis found herself taking a walk to just breathe. While minding her business, she was approached by another foreign gentleman, who'd introduced himself as Steve.

At this point, Phyllis was pregnant, tired, and not interested in anyone who seemed to be interested in her. Yet, this man walked and talked with her until she reached her destination. Then Phyllis realized that she, and her girls, had missed the bus, and it was going to be a while before the next bus arrived. As a courtesy, Steve offered to give them a ride to where they were going. She was too tired and exhausted from the day to allow her pride to speak for her. So, Phyllis accepted the offer.

When Steve dropped them off at the shelter, he told her to give him a call if she ever needed anything. She was in no position to date anyone. Phyllis just wanted to focus on rebuilding her life with her children. However, she noticed that this gentleman appeared different from her past lovers. He seemed to only want to put a smile on her face. She was honestly skeptical of his niceties. After living in a world where she had to be aware of everyone's hidden agenda, Phyllis found it hard to believe that he was "*just*" anything.

Phyllis later learned that Steve was an honest Guyanese man who was not involved in a life of crime and enjoyed the simplicities of the world. He spent most of his day building and renovating homes as a carpenter. He took pleasure in drinking a few cold Guinness or Heineken beers while shooting the breeze with close friends after work.

This was honestly refreshing for Phyllis. She reveled in the positive interactions. More importantly, she appreciated that he didn't judge her situation. He just helped where he could. Phyllis eventually accepted more of his offers, and his love for her and her children. She slowly started to believe that Steve was the additional support she needed to begin picking up the pieces to her life.

Then, after residing in a shelter for roughly three weeks, God granted Phyllis' prayer. The DC government assigned her a three-bedroom house, in the housing projects, on 57th street in southeast DC. It was not glamorous, but it was a place to create a home for her children. She was feeling hopeful again. In her excitement, Phyllis was sure to keep her integrity with her prayer. She informed Steve that he, or any other man, was not invited to live with her and her children. Steve understood and respected her wishes. He didn't allow her request to interrupt his relationship with her.

It slowly became clear to Phyllis that Steve was really into her. She decided that she would lay all her cards on the table up front. She informed him that she was legally married to a man who wouldn't grant her a divorce. Phyllis told him that she was pregnant by a different man who was being detained until his deportation date. Most importantly, she let him know that her main priority was getting her life on track and taking care of her children.

This gentleman simply said, "Okay."

Phyllis was not expecting that response. She was used to fighting to prove her point. She often felt combative in her communication with Timmy. Then, she felt misunderstood in her delivery with Checko. Naturally, Phyllis was waiting for the follow-ups, but they never came. This felt too good to be true, so Phyllis began to brace herself for the moment Steve would reveal his hidden agenda.

This was the late 1980's, and men appeared very different from the men in her father's generation. Because of the heavy drug influence in the city and the events of her past relationships, Phyllis was guarded. She couldn't believe that there was nothing he wanted from her. More importantly, Phyllis often wondered why Steve wanted to be in her life. With all the baggage that she carried; she didn't believe that he simply wanted her.

Nonetheless, Steve didn't allow her doubt to influence his generosity. He helped furnish her home with beds for her daughters. He also drove her to the detainment center to visit Checko, took her on dates, and even paid for sitters whenever needed. Yet, no matter how much Steve did for her, she was sure to keep enough distance to protect herself from falling victim to similar situations in her past. However, that didn't last long.

A month or so after her 27th birthday, Phyllis gave birth to her fourth and final child. And as we now know, I am that child. Although I arrived earlier than she expected, she was in the space of accepting that God would make everything work together for her good. Even though she couldn't see it at that moment. There were so many things happening at once. She'd just let Timmy sign his name on her daughter's birth certificate where Checko's name should have been, all while Steve was pursuing her heart.

While so many doors of men were open, Phyllis felt stuck in a closet full of skeletons. My father, Checko, was in a cell without knowledge of my arrival. Meanwhile, my mother's husband, Timmy, was still questioning whether I was his child. Enough was enough! This was no way to rebuild or start over.

Within weeks of my birth, my mother finally revealed her truths. She unhooked her husband by informing him that he was not my father. Then, she did the thing that scared her the most. On her final visit to see my father, she told him about my name. Just as she expected, both men were devastated by the news. However, she was free of the burden.

Then, to her surprise, Steve decided he would be my "father." He vowed to always be in my life, even if their relationship didn't work out. Then, just like that, Phyllis took down the walls and let Steve into her heart. Inevitably, Phyllis was back in a relationship.

We crave for others to release their judgements of us. Yet, the most hurtful judge we face is ourselves.

The heart is resilient and forgiving, it is the mind that causes us stress.

ALEXANDRA ELLE

Chapter Three:

Where Do I Belong?

Dom Skinner

It is now the early 1990s, and Phyllis, my mother, had found her footing. She began working again. Her house, in the projects, was feeling warm and homey. Her daughters were stabled. And to top it off, she was in a relationship with a man who was teaching her responsibilities on the legal spectrum, such as building credit and getting a valid driver's license.

Phyllis was feeling like she'd gotten her spunk back. They were going on romantic weekend getaways and shopping sprees. Together, they'd take my sisters and me on family vacations to the beaches and amusement parks. Though she was happy, my mother kept her word and did not allow Steve to move in with us.

During this time, I am a whole person with personality, language, and desires. As I am told, I was not your average toddler. I began walking at ten months. I was potty trained before my second birthday. And when I was three years old, I was telling anyone who would listen, "I am going to be a doctor when I grow up so I can save lives."

I was that kid that everyone would make comments about, like, "That girl has been here before.", meaning I was a reincarnation of someone who'd lived and passed away. Whether or not that is true, I believe my extraordinary manner was greatly influenced by my older sisters, Nekisha, Ashley, and Sade'.

I wanted to do everything my sisters were doing. I'd observe them closely then try it for myself. Most of the time, they thought I was a crazy child with no fears. There was nothing I wouldn't try. If I was told I could do it, I was going to prove you right. But if you said to me that I couldn't do something, I was going to work hard to prove you wrong.

My earliest memories are of my mother and sisters telling me to "sit down somewhere and stop moving." They quickly realized that I was nothing like my sister, Sade', who is just a year older than me. I was not going to pick up a barbie or toy to play with it. I was going to listen and observe everything around me. Then, I was going to join the conversation. Yes, I was entering the conversation as a toddler.

Well, mainly to ask a ton of questions to understand the context of their discussion. After they would laugh or giggle from being shocked, they would answer the first question and maybe the second. By the time I got to the third question, I was released to do whatever adventure I could imagine in my little brain.

My experiences often led to a broken item, someone getting hit by accident, or me falling down a flight of stairs and something else breaking. Nothing was off-limits in my mind. I was running from dinosaurs in a jungle, fighting off aliens, hiding from spies, and so much more. My adventures had me jumping off furniture, climbing on the railing to hide in cabinets, crawling between glass tables, and using barbie's legs as weapons. Needless to say, I got in trouble quite often.

Besides having an adventurous spirit, I can't remember much of my toddler years other than the stories others have shared with me over the years. My Aunt Hope loves to share a story about a night she was on babysitting duty while my mother and Steve were out on a date.

I was about two years old, and I wouldn't sleep until my mother came home. I was probably crying, so I think my aunt just let me do whatever I wanted. I went into my mother's room, which was against the rules in Phyllis' house. No one was allowed in her bedroom when she wasn't home. Even when she was home, she didn't want us in her room. But there I was, in the forbidden place, laying in her bed, just waiting.

Since there was no one in my mother's room with me, I started taking coins from the money jar and placing them under the pillow. Phyllis used to keep an empty water jug in her room and fill it up with loose coins and dollars. In my little mind, there were enough coins in it to fill up a treasure chest, and it was an adventure trying to get the cash to escape the slim opening of the jar. I'm not sure if I planned to keep the coins for later or if I was in one of my imaginary worlds. Either way, I wasn't really good at it.

Phyllis entered her bedroom and witnessed what I'd done, and she went off. First, she cursed out my aunt because I wasn't asleep. Then, she yelled at me for the coin situation. I laid back with my arms up and hands behind my head, totally unbothered. I was just happy that she was home.

In her frustration, she said to me, "I'm going to beat your butt."

Without hesitation, I responded, "No, you're not."

Of course, everyone was in total shock because Phyllis was not the soft and cuddly type of woman. When she yelled or made a threat, she usually made good on her promise. My Aunt Hope laughed at the strange situation but was actually afraid for me. Because Phyllis was also in total disbelief at my response, she made a slight giggle and told me to go to my room. This was one of many of my "What did she just say?" moments.

What I remembered most about my toddler years was asking for my mother. I remember crying for hours and saying, "I want my mommy." My sisters hated it.

Sometimes, Nekisha would hold me in her lap and rub my ears until I calmed down, or she'd give me a snack when she didn't want to be bothered. I was a greedy little monster, so a snack would often do the trick. My sister, Ashley, would distract me by engaging me in games that weren't really games.

Ashley would say, "Let's play 'school.'"

She knew how to take advantage of how much I wanted to go to school like them. I thought school was a real game, and I wanted to win.

She would always say, "Ok, I'm the teacher, and you and Sade' are the students."

Ashley would have us calling out colors, shapes, letters, and numbers. I really thought the flashcards were games. When Sade became bored and left us to play in her dolls' hair, Ashley would make me practice writing our phone number or address. While she was trying to keep me from crying, Ashley unknowingly put me ahead of every three-year-old I would soon share a class with.

I enjoyed playing 'school' so much that hours would pass by without me asking for my mother. Before I knew it, Nekisha was making us eat dinner and putting us to bed. However, there were plenty of times my mother would return home earlier than expected, and it would make my day. Even if it was for her to rest before her next plan for that evening, I didn't care.

We all were once a child. And every child cries out for their mother.

Too Young to Understand

By the time I was five years old, I had realized the shift in my house. I believe this is the time Phyllis and my godfather, Steve, broke up. The truth is, I can't remember when it happened because he wasn't around often. I remember sometimes seeing him before I went to bed. He came to the house late at night or in the evening, typically after my bedtime. I would get excited when I saw his white pickup truck drive around the neighborhood circle and park in front of our house.

I would tell my sisters, "My daddy's here.", and run down the stairs, nearly tripping over my feet because I was moving so fast.

I would jump in his arms and start asking him a million questions before he could get through the door. Phyllis would always tell me to slow down. Our reunion never really lasted more than twenty or thirty minutes. But I was ecstatic every time.

Steve would ask me, in his thick Guyanese accent, "Are you being a good girl? Are you staying out of trouble?"

My answers were always, "Yes." Even if I'd gotten in trouble that day, I did my version of explaining how it wasn't really trouble.

Then, he'd say, "You know your daddy loves you, right?" and like a movie on repeat, I'd nod my head, he'd kiss my cheeks, digging in his pockets, and hand me a few dollars.

After that transaction, my mother would tell me that it was time to go to bed. But, before I walked up those stairs, I'd always ask, "When can I spend the day with you?"

There was always a response, but never an answer that involved a date. I think my mother knew the answer because she would faithfully interrupt before my follow-up questions.

Dom Skinner

My relationship with my godfather, Steve, seemed very transactional. When he told my mother that he'd always be in my life, I don't think he considered all the variables that came with his statement. When they'd met, my mother dealt with so much that she wasn't fully invested in a relationship with him. However, when she closed up the skeletons in her closet, and he willingly signed up to be a father figure to me, she went full in. Then, her unsettled baggage followed, which added tension to their relationship.

Events from Phyllis' previous relationships replayed in her memory and started to plant themselves in her current relationship with Steve. When her insecurities began to present themselves, the dynamic of their fun-filled relationship started to change. A missed call turned into accusations of cheating. A late arrival turned into an argument, and small arguments turned into physical altercations.

After years of breaking up and making up, they eventually called it quits. The man that promised to always be in my life moved on and married a sweet Guyanese woman. While he moved on from his relationship with Phyllis, he tried to maintain a relationship with me. I remembered meeting Steve's new wife and her sons. It was apparent that he wanted a smooth integration and for me to feel accepted in his family. I was excited to have more brothers. I already had an older brother from my godfather. Although I didn't get to see him much, I was hopeful that things would change.

Sometimes my mother would take me to their family's events. Sometimes she'd stay. Other times she'd just drop me off. I remember feeling like an outsider or sitting in a corner until someone came to speak to me. My older brother, Lil Steve, was much older than me, so he wasn't paying me any attention. Part of me wanted to go home where I was comfortable. But another part of me desperately wanted to belong.

Then, before I knew it, Steve and his wife were expecting their own daughter. My hope of belonging in this family began to fade. By this time, I was around eight years old and already feeling distant from everyone.

When it came to my godfather, I just told myself, "It's because he had his own family."

This belief grew stronger when I'd call and ask to spend time with him, and he'd respond with promises of stopping by when he could. And he would. It just wasn't very often because he owned a small construction company. When he wasn't fulfilling contracts, he was building the expansion of his house for his growing family.

Every time I would get sad about it, my sister, Sade', would say, "at least you have a godfather, and he gives you good gifts."

Which was true. Every time Steve came by, he brought a gift or handed me a few dollars for the ice cream truck. While many kids in my neighborhood didn't have fathers to receive gifts or money, I was never without resources.

There was nothing Steve wouldn't provide for me. Everything I asked for, he made a way for me to have it. But eventually, I didn't care about the things. I just wanted him to show up for me. I wanted to be enough for him to just spend some time with me.

Yet, once I heard that he and his wife were expecting a baby girl, I knew everything would change. And it did. I saw him even less, which later turned into just a couple times a year. To Steve and my mother, if I had everything I needed, I was fine. But neither of them could understand that what I truly needed was a hug.

The Three Men

Throughout my life, I knew the truth about my biological father, Checko. I am not sure when the information was given to me. But I would like to assume that I knew before I was five years old. I was aware that the man I called "daddy" was my godfather. Yet, during that time, I never referred to him as "godfather." He was just my father, because he told me that I would always be his kid. However, over the years, I wasn't able to view myself as a priority in his life. So, reminding myself that I was his godchild allowed me to feel less neglected.

I would tell myself, "It technically isn't his obligation to show up for me every time I call."

As for Checko, he would call from Jamaica, from time to time. He wouldn't say much. He'd just ask how I was doing. It was always awkward because I didn't know what to say to him. I always felt like I was talking to a stranger for the two minutes my mother would allow us to speak. Calling cards were expensive, and she didn't want us to eat up all the time before she could have an adult conversation with him.

In addition to feeling like an outsider with Steve's family and only speaking with Checko for two minutes a few times a year, I was constantly faced with questions about my last name. Of my mother's four daughters, all but one carries the name Skinner.

My oldest two sisters are proud to be called Skinner and loved spending time with their father's family. Their grandmother, Mrs. Skinner, is the sweetest lady. When she'd pick up her granddaughters, Nekisha and Ashley, she'd allow me and Sade to join them. She always made us feel welcomed in her family.

However, someone would always decide to guess which girls belong to the Skinner family. Everyone truly believed it was three of the four. But, if their father, Timmy, was around, he was sure to correct and state that I was not his child. I am not sure if he was still hurt by how my mother deceived him during her pregnancy with me or because he was paying her child support for three children instead of two.

When Phyllis decided to come clean to Timmy about me, she never thought twice about telling anyone anything different. When she took him to court for child support for his daughters, he contested. But the judge made it very clear that he would pay for every child she births, even if he isn't their father, until he grants her a divorce. I am not sure if he believed the order or if he didn't care. Phyllis didn't become legally single until I was eight years old. Even then, her now ex-husband was ordered to pay her child support for me.

No one ever had anything ill to say about Timmy because he didn't seem like a terrible man. He also wasn't mean towards Sade or me'. If my mother asked him to look after us when he picked up Nekisha and Ashley, he would. He even brought us snacks and treats when he came by the house.

Yet, my heart was ripped from my little chest every time I heard him say, "She's not my child."

While I knew it was true, it didn't stop my feelings from being bruised. I started to hate it when people asked me if I was related to someone they knew with my last name.

I would grudgingly say, "I'm not a Skinner."

It also didn't help that our family referred to us as "The Skinner girls." This would tear me up inside. My sister, Sade', often reminded people that she was not a Skinner, and her last name was Dunn. I was so jealous. I had no evidence to use when I wanted people to stop associating me with a name I wasn't accepted into.

Dom Skinner

I remember being so angry one day and asking my mother, "Why is my last name Skinner?"

She responded, "Well, my last name is Skinner."

As I said before, I was not a child to accept simple answers. I am observant, and I say what's on my mind. So, I followed up with, "Well, your last name was Dunn, but you married a Skinner. I understand why Nekisha and Ashley have that name. But their father isn't my father, so why do I have their last name and not your maiden's name or my father's last name like Sade'?"

Yep, I was the kid that would give you facts and ask you to rethink your answer. Phyllis knew I was not going to drop the topic. She thought of a solution that I couldn't verify myself.

"You and Sade were born in different hospitals. In Maryland, where I gave birth to your sister, the hospital allowed parents to choose any last name for their child. But you were born in DC, and the child had to be given the name of their mother if the father was not present to sign their birth certificate.", she concluded.

Because I was blessed with Phyllis' detective-like tendencies, I did not allow the conversation to end with that answer. I continued to ask questions.

"So, on my birth certificate, is my father's name on it?"

She replied, "No."

I followed up, "well, what does it say?"

My mother looked me in my face and said, "It just says N/A. Your father was being deported, so he couldn't be there. I didn't want to name you Skinner, but I didn't have a choice."

I had no way of verifying this information in my six- or seven-year-old body. So, this is the story I told everyone that asked me, "Why is your last name Skinner and Sade's name is Dunn if y'all have the same mother and father?"

Imagine being in elementary school telling other elementary-aged kids this story. It was unnecessary and only required a "mind your business" response. But the truth is, I was trying to convince myself more than anyone else. I was battling with worthiness at a young age. It was challenging being told that I didn't belong or feeling like I didn't belong.

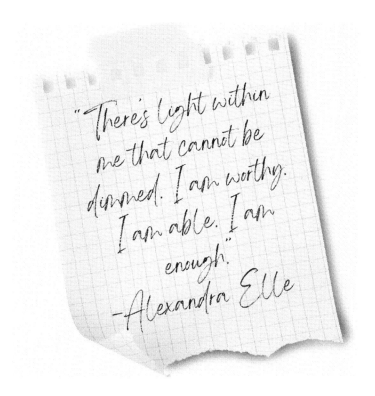

"There's light within me that cannot be dimmed. I am worthy. I am able. I am enough."
—Alexandra Elle

Words mean more than what is set down on paper. It takes the human voice to infuse them with a deeper meaning.

MAYA ANGELOU

Chapter Four:

Parents Don't Get a Handbook

Dom Skinner

Phyllis worked multiple jobs throughout my elementary school years to live up to the vow she'd made back in 1980. This time she was a single mother trying to keep that promise for four children. However, the tasks that came along with the pledge were accompanied by many challenges and plenty of stress. Phyllis didn't expect to be doing it alone.

Her schedule was busier than ever before, causing her to spend less time at home with my sisters and me. Phyllis was spending every waking hour grinding to make ends meet while also trying to have a life of her own. This wasn't as easy for her as it was for other women in their early 30's. So, smoking a pack of Newport cigarettes a day gave her the piece of calm she needed to survive. While crack cocaine and heroin were still the drugs of choice for many people in DC, my mother clung to Newport for her temporary release of stress.

The late 1990s was much like the '80s. Drugs were still plaguing the city, and crime was at an all-time high. Because we lived in the projects, my mother's priority was to make sure the inside of our home didn't reflect the neighborhood. She had clear rules; no one was allowed in her house when she was not home, at all. She expected us in the house at a specific time, with the doors locked.

Phyllis' days started early and ended late, which meant there were many days she'd head to work before we were awake and returned when we were asleep. But no matter the time she arrived home, our curfew was non-negotiable. Most nights, she'd call the house phone to make sure we were home. If we didn't answer, she'd plan for someone to come by the house to check on us. Yet, we knew better. We answered or called right back.

This rule also extended to her front or back porch. She would remind us that her porch was not a hangout spot, so our friends couldn't linger there. Phyllis spent so much time working that she wanted to feel like she was in her own sanctuary when she walked into her home. She wanted order, peace, and quiet. Everyone in my neighborhood was aware that my mother didn't tolerate people lingering on her porch.

If someone was on her porch when she pulled up to the house, she was not polite about telling them to leave in the boldest Patwa. I would hear people in my neighborhood say, "Yo, Jamaicans are crazy. I'm not messing with Ms. Phyllis. Y'all better not go on her porch."

One of her most important rules was, "just because we live in the hood doesn't mean we should act like we're hood." People have preconceived notions about folks who live in low-income communities or the projects. Media and other influences have led the world to believe that people who reside in such neighborhoods are ill-mannered, unruly, lacking integrity, lazy, and the list goes on.

Phyllis knew how the world expected her to appear. As a result, she worked hard to prove them wrong. Phyllis grew up with enough labels and was tired of others defining her. She earned respect in any room she walked into, with her head high and chest up. She could hold a conversation on any topic, and her clothes were impeccable. While this wasn't enough to shift her tax status, it was enough to teach her daughters what was possible when you don't allow your neighborhood to define you.

These rules were not merely suggestions. Phyllis meant every word of it, especially the rules about people in her home or on her porch. Yet, the rule about "acting hood" was often forgiven if the reasons were sufficient because she also had tendencies of going off on anyone who posed a potential threat to her or her family.

But, for the most part, she worked hard to present her best self, and we'd get in all types of trouble if we didn't do the same.

One of Phyllis' favorite sayings was, "You are a reflection of me, so do not go in there embarrassing me. Stand up straight."

While she is funny and easygoing with her friends, she is bold and direct with her children. Phyllis didn't have patience for nonsense. She would tell people that she was on a mission to raise us up right, which meant she was not interested in being our friends.

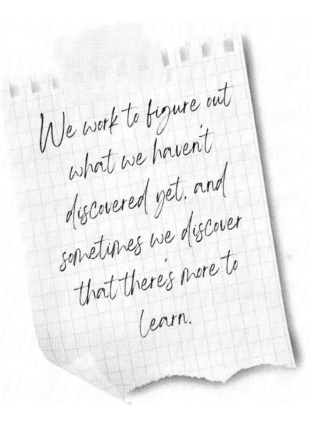

We work to figure out what we haven't discovered yet, and sometimes we discover that there's more to learn.

Dom Skinner

Figuring It Out

As I'd mentioned before, most of the stories people shared about me as a child were of me asking for my mother, crying for my mother, or simply waiting up until she returned home. I can't remember my mother sitting and holding me, watching a movie with me, or reading me a story. When I would ask for these things, she'd refer me to my older sisters.

So, Nekisha and Ashley stepped in quite a bit. Nekisha didn't mind me curling up next to her while listening to her newest albums or watching her favorite TV shows. Because of this, I knew every word of Usher's My Way album and every other R&B album of the 1990s.

Ashley was my movie-watching go-to. Although Ashley would get mad that I asked questions throughout the entire movie, she always invited me to watch another one with her. She loved watching The Five Heartbeats and The Temptations with me because I would sing and perform every scene.

Although I can recall countless moments shared with my sisters, I don't have many memories of quality time with my mother. I only remember wanting her. However, she was discovering her own wants and desires. In this balance of parent, provider, and single woman, Phyllis was also figuring out how to break a few generational cycles she fell victim to. She shared many stories of her aspiration to be different from her mother.

Phyllis didn't want us to find out about sex, drugs, or anything that could derail our futures from the world. Her mother wasn't open with her about navigating the world. As a result, she had to figure it out through many missteps. Phyllis believed it was essential for us to have direct knowledge from her. In her words, "The streets will not raise you."

Additionally, she never wanted her oldest child to feel responsible for caring for her younger children. Phyllis also

40

believed that children should be rewarded for their actions, education should be a top priority, and exposure outside of our neighborhood was essential. These were a few things that would have made her upbringing more favorable.

However, experiencing motherhood was different than she expected, so some of her aspirations fell short. One, in particular, was requiring her oldest child to care for her younger daughters in her absence. Phyllis was on a mission because she had "four daughters and no man to help raise them," as she would say. So, grinding to increase her income was her default. Also, she was still a young woman who wanted to enjoy her life, so she made time to go out with her friends.

Nonetheless, Phyllis gave everything she had in accomplishing the other areas. Phyllis gave gifts on every holiday. On Valentine's Day, she purchased us jewelry. On Mother's Day, she took us out. And the list goes on. While she was an excellent provider, gift-giver, and educator of the world, she held grades to the highest standard. We never actually talked about what we were learning in school. Although when I would try to share, she just wanted to know about the grades. Our school percentages would tell her if we were living up to her expectations for us.

As we all know, I was desperate for her to show me some attention, so all I cared about were grades. I needed all the gold stars. I wanted my teachers to write 100% as big as possible, so I could say, "Look, mommy! I got another A!" This would make her smile, then it was back to business as usual.

Grades weren't the only thing Phyllis rewarded. Keeping the house to her cleaning standards was non-negotiable, and we were given incentives to keep it up. But for Nekisha, the reward system looked different. When Phyllis felt shamed or rejected after countless attempts to secure stable childcare, she started leaning on her oldest kid for help. As a result, Phyllis gave Nekisha whatever she wanted, within reason, of course. Part of

Nekisha's incentives had her two favorite cousins, Shawnetta and Kelly, over all the time.

This became more of a relief to my mother than it was an incentive for Nekisha. She was still responsible for caring for my other sisters and me. Nekisha just had Kelly and Shawnetta around to keep her company. The more my mother allowed my cousins to spend time at the house, the more hours she spent out.

Nekisha, Kelly, and Shawnetta did a great job keeping me out of their way and crying about my mother. Kelly would make our food because she had skills like everyone's southern grandmother, and Nekisha would extend our playtime. But, consistent in my ways, I would still stay up past my bedtime waiting for Phyllis' arrival. Eventually, my mother became annoyed with me staying up late, and I started to get in trouble. She would yell at me and sometimes spank me. Nekisha tried saving me from those butt whippings plenty of times. But I was stubborn and wanted my way.

At some point, Nekisha took matters into her own hands. She'd let me play so hard that I didn't have the energy to stay up. I would crash immediately after my shower. But I got clever. I started to call my mother's pager or cell phone and asked her to come home. I wasn't always successful. Kelly would snatch the phone from me so quickly.

"Come on, Moonk. Leave Phil-skill alone, man. Go outside and play. She'll be home soon.", Shawnetta would say in her smooth, non-aggressive tone.

I didn't realize that I was on the verge of messing up their good time. Nekisha, Kelly, and Shawnetta enjoyed the freedom. They were living the teenage dream, and I was too busy being a brat to recognize it. I'm happy they never held that against me, though.

Getting In Where She Fits

Washington, DC has its own unique music genre, called Go-Go. The music involves a lot of bass tones and percussions. People around the country are familiar with the sounds of Go-Go music from the Godfather of Go-Go, Chuck Brown, and his #1 hit on the Billboard charts, Bustin' Loose, in the late 1970s. Since then, Go-Go music continued to evolve, and more bands around the DC area were formed.

During Nekisha's sixteenth birthday, my mother asked what she'd wanted. Every year Phyllis gave Nekisha a birthday party that everyone made plans to attend. Ashley, Sade', and I would sneak downstairs to sit at the bottom step, just to witness the teenagers dancing. Within minutes, we'd get caught and were forced back upstairs.

But this birthday, Nekisha was turning sixteen, and she'd hit some significant milestones in Phyllis' eyes. She was still doing well in school, she took care of me, Sade', and Ashley every time my mother asked, and most of all, she wasn't a teenage mother. Phyllis wanted this birthday to be unique for her, and so did Nekisha. So, without hesitation, Nekisha asked for a massive party at the recreation center, and she wanted the local band, High Performance, to perform.

While Phyllis was a fan of the music, she didn't know the first thing about booking a band for a party. However, it didn't stop her from figuring it out. Phyllis would win it every time if there was such a thing as a "Figure It Out" award. This woman has a gift of making things happen. Phyllis would put her pride aside every time if it meant she could make a miracle happen for my sisters and me. She will yell, fuss, and curse, but when it's all said and done, she will come through.

And like a mother on a mission to give her child everything she didn't have; she secured the band and organized the best Sweet Sixteen birthday celebration the neighborhood had ever seen. As Nekisha, Kelly, and Shawnetta tell it, everyone was talking about this party for years.

A few days after the big birthday bash, the lead rapper of High Performance invited Phyllis to a meeting, where the band asked if she'd be willing to manage them. They were impressed by how she'd pulled together Nekisha's birthday party and thought she had the skills and characteristics their band needed.

Before you knew it, Phyllis joined a band organization with other bands' managers and started managing the band, High Performance. She was working at her job during the day and rehearsing with her band in the evenings. When they weren't at a rehearsal, some band members planned and scheduled their performances at our house.

Phyllis was fully committed to their vision. She was dedicated to making this band known throughout the city. She even booked them shows out of town, which was a big deal in the '90s. Some of the more popular bands had never traveled outside the city at that point, and her new band was going places.

Of course, my sister and cousins were living the dream. They were getting into all the clubs and parties, and they were around band guys all the time. My mother also seemed to be finding joy in the entertainment world. She was feeling alive again. Meanwhile, I was getting in more trouble. My outspoken and adventurous personality was no longer tolerable with my mother.

Phyllis used to tell us that it was essential to ask questions when we didn't understand. She told us that it was silly to sit in ignorance. While she was referring to a classroom setting, I thought it also made sense to ask questions outside of the classroom. So, I did; to her. I was often told to "stay out of grown folks' conversations" or "Go outside and play" when I tried to engage with her.

So, when she was home, I spent most of my time playing outside and out of her way. But in my neighborhood, playing often led to fighting. So, I fought a lot. If I wasn't outside jumping off gates, playing catch football along with the basketball court, or fighting, I was in the house getting in trouble for one thing or another. Getting in trouble in my house didn't include a "time out" corner or being grounded from games or television.

In my house, Phyllis was pulling out a belt or swinging her heavy hand across your body. She didn't have time for the indirect lessons. Phyllis wanted us to know that she meant business. "I brought you into this world, and I will take you out." was a mantra that reminded us of how far she'd go to straighten us out.

As I mentioned before, she was not a patient woman, so this happened pretty often. The more she felt stressed, the more impatient she became, which led to a more aggressive disciplining. Eventually, I learned to calm down and reserve my words.

More importantly, Phyllis rarely had to handle me outside of the house because of my school or public behavior. I truly believed that she would have taken me out, and the last thing I wanted was for it to happen in public.

Parents are people who also want to have some fun, some adventures, and some parent-free time.

45

The Crying Stopped

By the time I was around nine or ten years old, Nekisha had moved into her own apartment, and my next sister, Ashley, became the lead babysitter of the house. Phyllis was still involved in the Go-Go band world, although her band had split up. She spent her free time helping her good friend, Ms. Marguerite, with events for the Backyard Band.

At that point, I was used to her unusual schedule, and I expected her absence. I slowly began giving up on a relationship with her. She spent more time yelling, fussing, and hitting us when she was home than anything else. Phyllis would get upset about the most minor things. She would yell at us if we didn't hear her whisper from downstairs. She'd wake up the entire house in the middle of the night if someone left a cup in the sink.

"Oh no y'all didn't leave dishes in my sink. Do y'all want rats and roaches in this house? Somebody better get down here and do these dishes."

This was her reaction to a cup and spoon. My sisters and I still joke about leaving one cup in the sink. Having a mother as extreme as Phyllis, sometimes it was best to laugh to avoid a constant headache. But some of her antics were not funny. One, in particular, was going shopping. I despised this more than anything.

Phyllis would get excited about getting us a new wardrobe for the upcoming season. Then, like clockwork, she'd fuss at us because she spent more money than she expected to. Phyllis never missed an opportunity to remind us of her hard work and sacrifices. Her speech would get louder and longer if one of us decided to complain, smack our teeth, or roll our eyes. I was always guilty of all three.

With her constant fussing, I started to believe that Phyllis just didn't like being a mother. Plus, with my "matter of fact" demeanor, she definitely didn't like me. Yet, on the contrary, she'd tell my teachers and all her friends how proud she was when I earned awards.

"That's my baby. I'm so proud of her". Phyllis would kiss and hug me after I was complimented on my achievements.

Yet, I didn't feel the same level of love and affection in our home. This made me feel like she was putting on a show. At home, she was always too tired or frustrated to listen to anything I was excited about. I would try to share my enthusiasm about a new accomplishment in class or a recent activity I was involved in, and she would dismiss me.

"Please. Not now. I don't want to hear about any more programs you want to join. Focus on one thing. You're going to be a jack of all trades and a master of none."

It used to hurt my feelings. So, I stopped sharing as much. I honestly started losing my desire to be around her. Eventually, the more she fussed, the more I tuned her out. Or at least I tried. Some of her comments lived in my mind, rent-free.

Between her hurtful words and the beatings, I began to wish I was never born into her family. I felt like no one saw my pain or cared. Instead, the adults around me praised my mother for the beautiful job she was doing. With every compliment they gave her, I slowly started to believe that I wasn't worthy of love. I wanted to live anywhere but with her.

"I wish I lived in Jamaica with my father." I blurted out after an episode of avoiding her belt.

Before I knew it, she packed up our bags and sent us all on a plane to Montego Bay, Jamaica. To be honest, I had no genuine interest in living in Jamaica. I didn't really know my father. The hidden truth was, I wanted to be anywhere, with anyone who wanted me around. In short, I desired to be wanted.

First Time in Jamaica

The time had come for me to put a face to the mysterious voice on those long-distance phone calls. I was going to meet my father for the first time, and my sisters and godsister, Shadaryl, were all with me. My mother decided to just send us and stay home in DC. This wasn't totally unusual.

Every summer, Phyllis would send us away, for weeks at a time, to different family members in other states, from North Carolina to Georgia, to Ohio, and to any cousin or grandparent that was willing to take us off her hands for a week. If we weren't in a summer program or sport or at an away camp, we were out of Washington, DC.

Although I was excited about this trip to Jamaica, I was beyond nervous. I'd never heard stories about Jamaica because Phyllis had never been. I only knew that it was a beautiful island and they spoke Patwa. Patwa is an English-based creole language, and Phyllis speaks it very well.

For most of my childhood, she spoke more Patwa than she did English. So most people, who didn't know her before 1988, believed she was Jamaican. She also cooked Jamaican food more than American food. My household was a true Jamaican home, and the only Jamaicans in it were me and my sister, Sade'. Yet, neither of us had ever been on the island until this unforgettable three-week trip.

We flew with an airline called Air Jamaica. It's no longer around, but I thought it was lovely. All the flight attendants had beautiful Jamaican accents and were so kind, plus all the food was Caribbean dishes. This was my first time on an airplane, so I didn't have anything to compare it to. All I know is, I was in heaven. Also, I was used to sitting for long road trips, so the five-hour flight didn't annoy me. I enjoyed every moment of it. Until the plane landed.

Let's Talk

When the plane wheels touched the pavement, my heart dropped to the bottom of my toes. My excitement turned into worry and doubt. So many thoughts rushed through my mind. "What if my father doesn't like me? Does he like hugs? Will he talk to me? I wonder if he's kind." My mind was going a million miles an hour. I was about to spend three weeks with a stranger, and the biggest worry in my mind was, "what if he's mean?"

Phyllis had a way of telling stories of her past relationships. I never remember what would prompt her to begin speaking about the things she'd experienced. However, I've heard the stories so many times that I could mimic her stories, word for word. Phyllis often shared how much she loved my father, Checko, then she'd follow up with how he was physically abusive during their relationship. I often overheard her talking about her fear of my father not sending us back if she allowed us to visit.

Phyllis told us that he was the only man she knew who wanted all his children living with him. While she would give us the details of some of their interactions, I couldn't help but get lost in my imagination of what it would feel like for a parent to fight for my presence.

Then, my daydream would become disrupted by my contradicting thought, "If he loved his kids so much, why didn't he fight his way back to America so he could raise me?"

All my mother's stories and my unsettling thoughts started rushing through my mind as the plane sped along the pathway, trying to come to a complete stop. My heart felt like it was pumping out of my chest like the cartoons. Then, I looked at all my sisters, and I felt a sense of calm.

While neither of them appeared calm from the unexpected feeling from the plane landing, my heart was at ease knowing that they were with me. No matter what I was about to experience, Nekisha was going to make sure I was okay.

Then, the airplane door opened, and the thick Caribbean heat poured into the plane. It was real. We were finally in Jamaica. After going through baggage claim and customs, we made our way towards the waiting cars, the loud horns, and the crowds of tourists and Jamaican natives.

I believe this was when I knew I didn't like large crowds. I was so uncomfortable with groups of people bumping into each other trying to get to their locations. Yet, I was also curious, so I stared at everyone. At times, my sisters had to call my name so I could pay attention to where they were moving.

Then, my father arrived. Nekisha spotted him immediately. Maybe because she was the only one who remembered or knew how he looked. He was short, slim, and bald, with a big smile and gap between his teeth similar to mine. His skin was lighter than caramel, and his eyes were soft hazel. I'm not sure what I was expecting, but this was not it.

He grabbed some of our bags and directed us to a van while some other gentleman helped him with the rest of the luggage. When we climbed into the van, a random woman and little girl, who appeared to be around 3 years old, were already sitting on one of the three rolls. The little girl, in her thick Jamaican accent, said, "mi sistas!"

I immediately knew that she was the younger sister, Tia, that my mother told me about. I assumed the woman, who appeared to be as young as Nekisha, was her mother. I soon discovered that the woman was not Tia's mother but my father's girlfriend. However, she was only a few years older than Nekisha.

This woman was not very welcoming. There was something about her energy that didn't sit well in my spirit. However, just like my Grandmother Helen, Phyllis didn't allow disrespect. So, I was polite.

Once we all piled up in the van, the driver made his way to our destination. Each of us took turns saying a few words or making a few statements. But most of the drive, we stared out of the window at the island. The drive didn't seem long, but it was very eventful.

During this time, the country hadn't developed all its roads. So, the ride would go from smooth to bumpy to smooth again. Dogs and cows were walking along the road, and people were selling fruit, sugar cane, and nuts at multiple intersections. I couldn't take my face away from the window. My father watched us in amazement.

When we finally arrived at our destination, we were greeted by so many people in the parish. Both family and friends of theirs. There were so many smiles as we walked from the road to my father's house. We weren't there for more than five minutes before we heard a woman's voice yell through the house, "Keith!"

My father just smiled without answering, as if he knew she was coming through the door anyway, and she did. She stormed through the door, asking if her nieces had arrived. With the biggest smile and most profound brown skin, this woman walked past my father and screamed with excitement as she laid her eyes on us. There was another woman, with similar features but a lot taller, that followed in behind her. She just smiled and watched.

We were excited because they were excited. But we clearly had no clue who these women were. Well, except Nekisha and Ashley. They knew the face of the first lady that walked in. She made statements about how big they'd gotten since she'd seen them. Both ladies hugged us tightly, checking our faces and making statements about which family member we resembled.

Eventually, my father came into the room and told us that the two women were his twin sisters, Peppy and Pauline. I knew that I had twin aunts, and I expected they'd look exactly alike, but they couldn't have been more opposite.

My sisters were familiar with my Aunt Peppy because she, and my other Aunt, Bev, lived in America while my father was there. But they'd never met my Aunt Pauline. So, she was meeting all of us for the first time. I was so amazed looking at how much Sade' and I resembled them as sisters. While Sade' and I are not twins, we appeared to be a younger version of them standing next to each other. Sade' was tall and slim like Pauline, and I was short and curvy like Peppy.

More family members, like Aunt Peppy and Aunt Pauline, came in and out to say hello and introduce themselves throughout the day. My first day in Jamaica was pretty exciting but very exhausting. Everything was different from our home in DC, but my father did his best to ensure we were as comfortable as possible. However, there was only so much he could do. Sade' and Shadaryl feared everything! They held each other's hands and went everywhere together. But this was their typical style. Sade' and Shadaryl were thick as thieves.

While Shadarly and I are closer in age, she and Sade' were more alike. She was the little sister Sade' wished she had. They were both gorgeous with thick long hair, and people reassured them all the time. They were also into boys and wearing cute outfits. I couldn't have been more opposite.

I was all about an adventure, so I didn't care what I had on as long as I could run and jump in it. The boys weren't checking for me. They saw me as their homie, Domo. I was faster and stronger than most of them, and I made sure they knew it. None of the boys thought that was cute. But I was always picked first to be on the kickball team.

During our first night in Jamaica, Sade' did not sleep until her exhaustion beat out her paranoia, which meant none of us slept. Because Jamaica is a tropical island, there are insects and lizards everywhere. Sade' squealed every time she thought she'd seen something crawling. Nekisha, Ashley, and Shadaryl eventually tuned her out. But, not me.

For some strange reason, Sade' and I had this thing where we'd try to go to sleep simultaneously. It was so weird. Throughout the day, we'd fight and argue like we barely knew each other. But, at night, in our shared bedroom, we didn't want to go to sleep if the other was still awake.

However, on this night, I was angry that I couldn't fall asleep, even after she was fast asleep and snoring on the other end of our shared bed. Before I knew it, the sun was up, and so was everyone else in the village. There was no way it was going to get any sleep.

The moment I tried drifting off to sleep to the sound of the birds chirping and the rhythm of the fan that was at the end of the bed, a neighbor yelled through the window, "Patrice! Let me borrow your clothespins, please."

When my father's girlfriend, Patrice, didn't answer, she continued calling her name until Patrice finally responded. The entire time, I thought, "this lady has no respect for the morning."

While I laid there trying to force myself to sleep, I heard people singing and talking, and the sound of water hitting the tin wash buckets. Then the smell of food started to flow through the room. In the midst of me trying to identify the spices in the air, my grandmother, Gi Gi, entered the room. She saw my eyes watching her, and she smiled. Her smile lit up the semi-dark room. I had no clue who she was, but I felt an instant connection to her.

I got up to meet her at the end of the bed where she was standing. She hugged me with so much intent that I just relaxed in her embrace. I'd never felt so safe and secure as I did in that moment. As I felt tears welling up in my eyes, I heard the sweet sound of my little sister's voice, "Gi Gi!"

I hugged her even tighter after hearing her name. At that moment, I knew exactly who she was. Tia jumped out of bed to join the hug. This woke up the room. Each of my sisters slowly began to open their eyes. Gi Gi tried to get Tia to lower her voice, but it was too late. Everyone was up.

I turned to Sade' and said, "this is our grandmother."

Like Tia and me, she jumped up to embrace her. After the introductions, Gi Gi told us to tell her what we wanted for breakfast. I think we asked for cereal, but she returned with mugs that were smoking hot and said, "drink."

This was my introduction to mint tea in the morning. Then, Tia, as her little helper, brought in bowls of porridge. My sisters and I looked at each other like, "this is not cereal." Gi Gi sensed the hesitation and told us to try it. It was divine! I was in sweet breakfast heaven. From that moment on, I tried anything she gave me. Well, except the bowl of chicken soup, with the chicken feet sticking out of the top. That creeped me out.

She, and Checko, paid attention to everything we said we liked and didn't like. Then, she made sure to bring us our favorites when she came over. But, most importantly, she made sure to give us so many hugs. Her hugs were magical. They made me feel like I was wrapped in a cloud of love. They were everything I'd forgotten I needed.

A few days into our trip, I finally met my father's oldest daughter, Stacy. She was younger than NeKisha but older than Ashley. From the time we arrived, everyone kept saying to me, "My God, you favor your big sister, Stacy."

I wasn't sure what to take from that. I didn't often hear that I was cute. I mostly received compliments about my grades or how well I was doing in one of my sports or activities. Because Sade' and I were close in age, we were often compared to each other.

Although no one, other than kids our age, ever said, "you're not as cute as Sade'," I felt it was implied when she was often told how beautiful she was.

54

Then those same people would look at me and say, "you're so smart." So, in my immature mind, I began to believe that I was not as pretty.

But, when I met my big sister, Stacy, I was mesmerized by her beauty. I thought to myself, "wow, y'all think I look like her?"

Her face was like our father's but feminine and softer, with a gap between her teeth and light caramel-toned skin. She moved lightly and poised. She appeared more polished than everyone else. But there was no doubt that Stacy was my father's daughter.

Besides having his features, she also carried his demeanor, observant and chill energy, but bold when she spoke. Although Stacy didn't talk much, I thought she was so cool. She no longer lived with our father, so we only saw her a few times during our time there. But I enjoyed every moment of it.

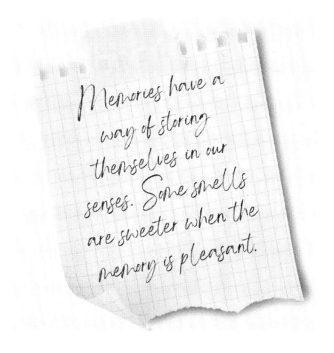

Memories have a way of storing themselves in our senses. Some smells are sweeter when the memory is pleasant.

Time With My Biological Father

My father! My father! I was finally meeting the man that I used to cry out for when Phyllis would beat me. This was the man I've heard countless stories about, from the beautiful love stories to the horrible nightmares. Phyllis shared it all. There I was, finally meeting Keith "Checko" Jones.

I remember thinking, "What would I say to him? I have so many questions." When we were all piled up in the van heading to his home, I felt shy. Me! Shy! That was even confusing to me. I was not a shy kid. I spoke to everyone about anything. But, for some reason, I felt like the cat had my tongue. Instead of speaking, I switched my gaze between the activities on the road to watching him watch us. From time to time, he would chuckle at our amazement. I felt his joy. He couldn't stop smiling, which made me smile.

Then, I heard him say, "My daughters are home."

I thought to myself, "Wow. This is our home. I have two homes."

For most of the days that we were there, Checko still had to go to work. So, we didn't spend every hour with him, like I'd hoped. While he was at work, it gave us a lot of time to spend with aunts and cousins. One, in particular, was my cousin, Romeo, who was extremely close to my father. Because of this, there was nothing he wouldn't do for him, which he extended to us.

Romeo took care of us. He made sure we knew about the newest music and how to do the dances, where to get the best beef patties, and he even climbed the trees to get us guineps. There was nothing Romeo wouldn't do to make sure we were enjoying Jamaica. He'd have us on the craziest adventures through the hills and mountains. We never knew what we would get into with Romeo, but I was always ready to follow him.

My father trusted Romeo but probably feared one of us would get hurt messing with Romeo's adventures. Checko also trusted us around his girlfriend, Patrice. This, however, I did not understand. From the time I met her, something didn't sit well in my spirit. While there were moments, she revealed a fun and caring side of her, most of the time, her energy exposed her jealousy.

Because I am my mother's daughter, I was blessed with her tendencies, such as observation. I'd spend time watching Patrice when she wasn't around my father. I wouldn't say much to her, and she didn't speak much to us. Most of the time, she just asked if we were hungry.

Phyllis told us when we were young, "don't eat from people you don't trust." So, collectively, my sisters and I would often say, "No, thank you."

My aunts saw the patterns, so they'd make sure we ate lunch while my father was at work. Most mornings, Checko cooked our breakfast before he headed downtown to his job. But, if he didn't, God sent one of my aunts or my lovely Gi Gi over to make us some porridge or saltfish, cabbage, and dumplings. Needless to say, my family wasn't too fond of Patrice, and she didn't seem to like them very much either.

Unfortunately, the family's disdain for Patrice only got worse when she made a mistake and assumed we didn't understand Patwa. One day, she and her friend were sitting on the front step when I walked by. She began to make derogatory jokes about my body. She even went on to add sexual remarks about why my body appeared so curvy.

I turned to look at her, knowing exactly what she said. She and her friend laughed. Then she says to me, "ay gal, ya alright?"

I didn't respond. I just looked at her. She and her friend continued laughing. Her friend agreed that I couldn't understand what was said.

I was livid. I was hot. But also, I knew it. My intuition was correct. I couldn't wait to tell my father. I didn't share it with anyone else, at the time, because I wanted to be the one to let him know that his girlfriend was a nasty woman. Unfortunately, I ended up playing myself to sleep before he returned home. I had no boundaries on how much energy I gave to playing.

However, I woke up early for my mission. I needed to tell him before he left for work. I'm not sure what time it was, but the sun hadn't made its entrance into the sky yet. I crawled out of bed slowly, trying my best not to wake Sade' and Shadaryl, since the three of us were sharing a bed. I tip-toed into my father's room to see if he was awake. I was praying that Patrice was still asleep.

To my surprise, I walked in to see my father near a small light or candle. It was glowing just enough to show that his eyes were slightly closed, and there was smoke coming from the ashtray. The smell of marijuana filled the room. He appeared to be praying, but his head wasn't bowed. Instead, it was slightly lifted towards the ceiling. I just watched silently, trying to understand what my eyes were revealing to me.

Living in Washington, DC, I've seen people use drugs in the alleyways or nodding off at the bus stop from a strong hit of cocaine or heroin. I was also familiar with the smell of marijuana. Unfortunately, my friends and I were skilled in identifying a drug by the aroma in the air. But what I was witnessing with Checko was different. I thought to myself, "Is this what Rastafarians do?"

Phyllis told us that our father, Checko, was a Rasta. Every time Sade and I wanted something that went against our father's beliefs, she was sure to remind us.

When asked if we wanted pork, Phyllis was quick to answer for us, in Patwa. "No, mon, them not eat pork. Checko a kill me if mi give him pickney them swine."

Let's Talk

I remember asking my mother if I could loc my hair, and her response was, "Ay gal, what you know 'bout dreads them? You don't know the meaning, so you can't do it. When you understand, then you can do it."

Talk about a frustrating conversation. First of all, why was Phyllis speaking in a riddle? Secondly, I was six years old. Of course, I didn't know the meaning of dreadlocks. No one ever told me there was a meaning. But I wouldn't be Dominique if I didn't ask her. Phyllis told me to ask my father. She knew I wouldn't, so the conversation was over.

While Phyllis never gave us full details of the culture, she trusted that one day, Checko would. What she did tell us was that our father believed in his customs. I was getting a small glimpse of my father for the first time, which told me more about who he was or what he believed. So, I stood in the doorway and watched.

I thought to myself, "Is this why he is always so majestic and calm?"

As I was imagining what he was saying in his mind, or when he moved his mouth to speak softly, he turned to meet my gaze.

He smiled almost as bright as the candle next to him. "Morning, mi daughter. Wah gwaan? Ya aight?"

After whispering my good morning and saying I was fine. Checko got up and headed to the kitchen, which was in a separate structure from the house. I put my slippers on and followed behind him. He didn't speak, neither did I. We just were.

Then he asked, "Do you want saltfish and dumplings?"

My colossal smile made him smile. The feeling of simply being made my world feel complete. I thought of nothing. I said nothing. I just watched him cook.

As I stood in the doorway watching, the sun started to come up, and the early risers began moving around the village. It didn't change my focus. He picked up one ingredient at a time and told me what it was, then chopped it up. After a while, he began our small talk, like "Are you enjoying Jamaica? Do you want to go to the beach? Does your mother make you dumplings at home?" etc.

While these questions were surface-level and straightforward, this felt like our first real introduction. But the moment was soon interrupted by the reason I woke up before the sun; Patrice. I heard her voice. "Keith, ya aight?" as she made her way from the house to the kitchen.

I immediately got upset with myself. "How did I get distracted? I was supposed to break them up."

She walked up, and I wanted to vomit. I moved out of the way, thinking, "If I told him. He probably wouldn't care. We're leaving in a few days anyway."

I think Checko felt my energy shift. A few minutes after I'd returned to the room that I was sharing with my sisters, he entered to ask if I was okay. Before I could answer, Tia woke up and interrupted my words with, "Daddy! Mi hungry."

While I could have spilled the beans on Patrice at that moment, I punked out and told him that I was okay.

Another day went by, and I said nothing about the statements Patrice made the day prior. My goal was to never speak to her again. But, later that day, while my father was out, Patrice was at it again. This time I overheard her saying similar remarks about my godsister, Shadaryl. Talking about her thick lips and her body structure.

I'd never wanted to fight an adult as much as I wanted to fight her. This time, I was not going to be quiet about it. She'd gotten too comfortable with speaking ill about children and laughing at what she thought was our ignorance. I told my sisters and Romeo.

To be honest, I wasn't sure what was going to happen. But before I knew it, my Auntie Bev and my sister, Stacy, were in the village asking me to tell them every word she said. I thought to myself, "Oh snap! What have I done? My words are about to get that woman killed."

My Auntie Bev is my father's oldest sister, and she doesn't play about her family. My mother would refer to her as "Bad Gal, Bev." Phyllis shared many stories about their time together in the 1980s. My aunt had a reputation for being a dangerous woman. She didn't like to fuss or argue. She and my father were similar in that regard. If she came for an altercation, she didn't come to talk.

On the contrary, I'd never seen my sister, Stacy, upset. As I mentioned before, she was so chill. But when she came to the village that evening, she was fuming.

While I was being questioned about every detail of Patrice's words, Checko arrived. He couldn't get out a proper "hello" before my Aunt Bev started in on him, in a proper big sister style. "Yo Keith! Why you sleep next to one nasty woman?"

My father was so confused. Then, Stacy started with her words. Before I knew it, he told them to leave because he didn't want that drama in his house. At no point did either of them tell him what I said. They were so mad that they only talked about how terrible Patrice was, but not the why.

The situation escalated quickly. The talking ceased as Aunt Bev and Stacy began charging at Patrice, while Checko did all he could to stop them. Eventually, he told Patrice that she had to leave. I was relieved that she didn't die and because she was gone.

I thought to myself, "Wow! He does care about me. Maybe I should have said something sooner. Maybe it wouldn't have gotten so messy."

Once she'd left and the rage from his home dissipated, Checko picked up his broom and began sweeping his floors. He appeared to be in a place of calm in comparison to everyone else. The folks outside were still talking about the drama. Meanwhile, Checko didn't speak a word. He didn't ask me questions about it, and I didn't share any details. To him, that moment had passed.

At this moment, I realized that my mother and father couldn't have been more different. They were like night and day. Checko appeared very different from the events my mother shared of their relationship. I'd never met a person so serene. Most of the time, he was quiet. My mother, on the other hand, was more like turbulence.

Things could get very uneasy depending on the events of her day. If there was chaos, she was not the calm in the middle of the storm. Phyllis would actively fight the winds until she worked herself into exhaustion and frustration. While she can find her calm, it takes some reinforcement from God and a friend, or two, to get her there.

Our first of many visits to our home in Jamaica was eventful, beautiful, and messy. We developed relationships with family, learned more about our culture, danced, swam in the ocean, traveled to different parts of the island, and ate so much good food. My grandmother, Gi Gi stole my heart. She was so feisty and unapologetic in her strength, and I loved every bit of it. I enjoyed watching her hand wash our clothes in a pail of soapy water. When she would catch me watching her, she'd say, "come, gal," while tapping her knee.

She'd sit me on her lap and hug me so tight and say, "My gal, you're going to be alright.", in her thick Jamaican accent. I never understood why she'd say that every time she hugged me. But eventually, I found myself holding on to her words.

When we left Jamaica, I felt complete. I finally received the missing puzzle to my life's story. I arrived back in DC with a new perspective and appreciation for everything we were blessed to have. I was also excited to hear my mother's voice again. I couldn't wait to share all of our adventures. She was also happy to listen to them. But the first thing she asked for was the mixed CDs my Aunt Bev sent for her.

Phyllis is a dancing machine, and nothing makes her body move like reggae music. When she put the first CD in the stereo system, my sisters and I started dancing and showing her the new moves we'd learned. Smiles and laughter filled our living room. We stayed up for hours just talking about every detail of the trip. When she found out about "the Patrice" situation, she went off. We had to reassure her that I was okay and that my father had gotten rid of her.

We were all on a Jamaican high for months. I was excited to tell my friends about my father in Jamaica. I started to speak more Patwa and asked Phyllis to make saltfish and dumplings when she was home. Then, my heart leaped out of my chest when my mother told us that Romeo was coming to live with us. I started telling everyone, "My Jamaican cousin is moving with us."

When he arrived, everyone was prepared for him. Friends and all. But I was not ready for the news he brought with him. My father and Patrice were back together, and my world was crushed.

I immediately felt insignificant. "How could he be with someone who'd said such terrible things about me?" "Does he not care about me?" "Of course, he doesn't. That's why he never fought for me like he fought for the rest of his children." These were all the thoughts that played on repeat for years.

My spirit was unsettled over the years of returning to Jamaica, and I felt like I'd lost the connection I thought I had with my father. When I heard that Patrice was pregnant, I cried and said, "Checko hates me. He probably doesn't even believe I'm his child. It's cool. I never have to go back to Jamaica. I don't need a father. I can't miss what I never had." I was already learning how to mask my feelings with narratives that made me appear unfazed.

Then, my Gi Gi passed away, and I was forced to confront my misery. I'd lost my favorite person on the entire island, and my heart was broken. By this time, Patrice was pregnant with her second child. We were all broken-hearted for one reason or another. Even Phyllis, who also traveled to Jamaica to pay our respects.

While everyone was celebrating Gi Gi's life, I felt like a piece of me was dying on the inside. I barely spoke to Checko, which probably seemed normal for him. But, for me, I was avoiding his presence. My heart was so hurt that I didn't want to meet my beautiful baby sister, Shantel. If I had it my way, I would have spent my entire week away from Checko's house and everyone in it.

I felt like I was suffering, and no one cared to see it. My Gi Gi would have seen it. She would have made me a cup of hot mint tea and hugged me until I felt better. But she wasn't there, so I had to hold onto her words, "My gal, you're going to be alright." Yet, I wasn't sure how, but I had nothing else, so I had to trust it.

After that trip, I began to feel less connected to Jamaica. Phyllis sent me, by myself, the following summer. That was the first time I went to Jamaica without Sade'. I thought I was going to be okay. I thought that I'd gotten past the betrayal. Plus, I honestly missed my family in Jamaica.

In my heart, this was going to be the summer I told Checko my feelings, and I would build a relationship with him. I was older. I was technically a teenager, and I'd spent days crafting up my speech in my head. But that speech never happened. Instead, on day five, of my two-week trip with my father, I had my bags packed, and I was headed to Stacy's new apartment. I spent the rest of my trip with her. When I called my mother to tell her I wasn't comfortable, Stacy was there within hours to pick me up.

Checko worked most of the time, and I refused to share energy with Patrice. My spirit still didn't sit well with her. When my father was home, he was busy making sure everyone was taken care of. Also, if I'm honest, he appeared happy, which made me sad. How could he be happy while I was feeling neglected and unvalued? Could he not see that his relationship with her was hurting me?

I didn't know how to have a conversation with him without saying, "Why don't you care about me?" So, I decided not to say anything. When my unsaid words started to suffocate me, I called my mother and asked her to send me home. That clearly wasn't going to happen. I was not about to waste her money, she reminded me. It wasn't like I was a drive away, and she could pick me up. I was going to have to stay until my scheduled flight.

But, as always, my mother, Phyllis, came through with the solution. Once she realized she couldn't convince me to stay at my father's, she called my big sister, Stacy, and arranged for me to stay with her. If nothing else, Phyllis will make a way for her daughters to be comfortable, even if she isn't there to do it herself. I'm not sure if she ever told Checko the whole truth about why I left. I don't think I cared to ask.

Additionally, I left Jamaica, never having a conversation with Checko. I'd decided, "If he didn't care, I no longer cared."

I boarded my flight with a heavy heart. While traveling home, I asked God, "Why did you give me to parents who never wanted me? Was I born to be a loveless child? What did I do to deserve this?"

As I stared out the airplane window, I allowed my mind to drift. Then, I smiled. I'd, unknowingly, finessed a whole week with my big sister. I went to a reggae club on the beach. Stacy snuck me into a casino just to eat jerk chicken because she thought the food there was great. I got a second ear piercing without my parents' permission. Most importantly, we spent hours, no days, having sister time.

While I was ready to throw the entire trip away because I couldn't recommit building a relationship with my father, something magical happened in its place. I developed a relationship with my big sister, Stacy. It was at that moment I remembered Gi Gi's words, "You're going to be alright." I was alright. No, I was better than alright. I knew I was loved. Maybe, like Phyllis, Checko was too focused on the "taking care of" that feelings weren't important. Maybe, I was too sensitive. Perhaps I was ungrateful. Maybe all of it was true, and I was still going to be alright.

When we hold on to our pain and resentment from our yesterday, our hands and hearts aren't open to receive the blessings of our today.

A Change in Culture

When Nekisha left the house, Phyllis trusted Ashley to follow Nekisha's path in maintaining the home in her absence. Nekisha and my mother had a special relationship and understanding. Phyllis listened to Nekisha differently than she did the rest of us. She was interested in hearing what she had to say.

While my mother often said, "I love all my girls the same," she definitely had different relationships with us.

Because Nekisha was the eldest and our fathers weren't around, Phyllis saw Nekisha as her partner. So that I am clear, she did not see her as her friend or equal. Phyllis made sure to always say, "I am not my children's friend.", and she meant it. While her relationship with Nekisha was complex, it was also sacred. However, when it came to Ashley, there were a lot of differences.

Ashley was born with terrible asthma. She was in and out of the hospital throughout her childhood due to breathing complications or asthma attacks. So, Phyllis was really strict about her playing outside. Between my adventure-influenced accidents and Ashley's asthma, Phyllis was a regular at Children's Hospital. She'd yell at us all the time about how tired she was of going to the hospital. But no one was as tired of the hospitals as Ashley.

Her asthma caused her to miss many school days, which affected her grades and motivation to be in school. While her classmates were moving ahead, she was left behind without proper tutors or educational assistance. Because Phyllis was narrow-focused on providing stability for us and having an adult life for herself, Ashley's education went unnoticed.

One of Ashley's teachers told my mother that Ashley needed to be placed in special education classes because of her test scores that school year. Ashley was already receiving speech therapy for a lisp, and her young teacher assumed it all was related.

Ashley didn't have a problem learning; she chose not to speak much in class because it was frustrating when she wasn't understood. But she loved to learn. However, her newly certified teacher refused to see the correlation between Ashley's missed school days, the effects of her medication, and test scores. Instead, she moved towards having Ashley labeled with a learning disability. Phyllis didn't know that she could have asked for a second opinion. Instead, she accepted the information as facts. Just like that, Ashley was labeled, and no one fought for an effective Individual Education Plan (IEP).

Phyllis left Ashley's intellectual journey up to DC Public Schools. She trusted the professionals, and unfortunately, they failed in their promise to help Ashley succeed. Once she was labeled, no one had faith in her abilities. Or at least this is what Ashley believed.

Their behavior didn't change, although Ashley spent most of her time helping her peers with their work. "She's such a great helper.", her special education teacher would report to my mother. Yet, she never said, "We should have her tested out.", and Phyllis never asked if it was possible. For as long as I could remember, Phyllis was hard on me about my grades. However, I never saw her push nor challenge Ashely in her academics. I guess, like Ashley's teacher, my mother lost faith as well.

By the time Ashley entered junior high school, she was tired of the hospitals, the treatment from her teachers, and the teasing from her peers. Phyllis, on the other hand, was just desperate for a solution for Ashley's lungs. Ashley was having asthma attacks, left and right. Luckily, her doctors finally decided she was old enough to try a different medication with a higher level of steroids.

The new medicine gave Ashley a new life, as well as a new body. She was no longer restricted to the house and outside became her playground. School, however, was not the place she wanted to be. She was already being shamed for being taken out of class to attend her special courses. Now, her new medicine had her pre-teen body transforming before her eyes. In months, Ashley's body went from skinny Minnie, like a toothpick, to a curvy girl with C-cup breasts. And the school kids had more to talk about.

Towards the end of Ashley's junior high years, she had gotten rid of her quiet girl persona. She started shutting down every kid with a big mouth, whether they were making statements about her or anyone who needed defending. Ashley, like the rest of us, is a fighter. Not just in spirit, but also in hands. Ashley became known for being quiet but lethal with her fist.

While she wasn't menacing, people in the neighborhood and her school began showing her respect. Her friends, however, took advantage of Ashley's new identity and called her whenever they were in a situation, and fighting was the resolution. Though she has the biggest heart and is sweet as pie, people viewed Ashley as a thug. While this isn't how she viewed herself, she allowed people to say what they wanted because at least she was outside.

When her reign over babysitting duties started, Ashley was making her start in high school. But, more importantly, she was enjoying the outside. She and her friends would travel all over the city, walking and taking the Metro bus wherever their adventures led them. While my mother's rules didn't change, the culture around and in our house did. Ashley created her own set of rules.

Because we were taught to stick together, Sade' and I, we're faithful followers of what Ashely told us to do and say. Most times, that included lying to our mother when Ashley left us in the house alone, to hang out past her curfew. I'm confident that this isn't what Phyllis meant, nor expected when she told us to always look after each other.

While I practiced the ride-or-die code of conduct, Sade' punked out a few times and went against the story or plan. She was afraid to experience one of Phyllis' extreme butt whoopings. My mother rarely hit Sade'. I, however, was used to them. But I wasn't used to being on my big sister's bad side, nor did I want to be. Ashley had helped me cover up many broken items and saved me from countless beatings. There was no doubt that my loyalty was to the sister gang.

Phyllis, on the other hand, was putting forth her best effort to have a life outside of working and parenting. She started dating again. Although Phyllis kept her vow and didn't allow men to stay at our home, this didn't stop her from spending nights out. And there were many.

However, she started making Sunday dinners. If she was busy with work, then out on Fridays and Saturdays, she was home on Sundays. Phyllis began to make it a routine. She never announced it. It just became a more consistent occurrence.

During this time, there were more unannounced occurrences. My older cousin, Delvon, moved in with us. One day, he was taking us bowling in his crappy car. The next day he was waking up from the couch asking me to make him breakfast. I was nine. From that day forward, I saw him every day.

He was no longer my big cousin. He was my big brother. He teased me. We threw punches. He allowed me to ride around with him while he listened to Jay-Z and Scarface albums. He gave me an allowance. And like a true older sibling, he cursed me out when I got out of line. I had two older siblings in charge again: Ashley and Delvon. But neither was effective in managing the house like Nekisha, Kelly, and Shawnetta.

Throughout my childhood, there was always someone living with us. Everyone came to my mother when they needed a reset. But when Delvon came, it was different. He was like the son my mother never had, and she treated him as such.

Delvon is a few years younger than Nekisha and a few years older than Ashley. But he was mature beyond his years. He wasn't lost or needed a handout, and Phyllis didn't feel like she was raising him. Delvon became somewhat of an additional help like she'd imagined her son would be.

Delvon had just gotten in trouble with his mother, but Phyllis had a soft spot for him. She was familiar with his choices. But, more importantly, she expected him to keep Ashley out of trouble, and me and Sade' in line. So, our home became his home.

Delvon was focused on his goal to hustle up enough money to pay for his engineering degree, so he wasn't paroling anyone. I'm not sure how much of this Phyllis knew at the time. But what she did know was that he would keep her house and daughters safe while she was out.

Delvon most definitely kept Sade' and me occupied. Though he gave us an allowance, we had to earn it. In addition to our chores, we had to wash his clothes, make him sandwiches whenever he asked for them, and not talk about any of his girls in front of his other girls. Easy peasy.

In the meantime, he and Ashley were tight. He took Ashley everywhere with him. When Ashley wasn't with Delvon, she was staying out late past her curfew with her friends. There were plenty of nights Phyllis would come home from a late work shift or after a band set with Ms. Marguerite, and find Sade' and me asleep. But Ashley was nowhere to be found. As any concerned parent would do, Phyllis would wake us up to ask about Ashley's whereabouts.

"Where is your sister?" she'd ask.

Pretending not to know what she was talking about or who she was referring to, I'd rub my eyes and swarm around in my bed sheets. "Huh? Who?"

71

"Get up, I know y'all know something.", Phyllis would start to elevate her voice. "Do y'all want something to happen to your sister? What if she gets hurt or murdered while she's out in those streets, and y'all not saying nothing?"

Sticking to the ride-or-die code of conduct, I'd stand firm in my false ignorance. "Ma, I don't know. She was in her room when we went to sleep. Right, Sade'?"

I'd wait for Sade' to back me up. My mother knew if the truth was going to come out, it would come from Sade'. But I trusted that Sade' was a loyal member of the sister gang. So, I peeked my head out from the bottom bunk, looking up, trying to get Sade's attention. Her long pause was a clear sign that we weren't on the same page. "Sade', you up?! Tell ma."

I could hear Sade' shifting in her bed above me. "Yea, ma. We were sleeping. We don't know where she is?" Sade' would finally say.

"I'm going to ask y'all one more time. Where is your sister?" Phyllis would say in her calm, stern voice.

Standing my ground, I'd sit up to make it more believable, "Ma, we really don't know where she is. She was in her room."

Walking away, Phyllis would make her threat, "Let me go get my belt since y'all like lying. I guess I'll have to beat the truth out of y'all."

"Ma, we're not lying!" I'd say before Sade' could cave on the story.

Sade' would whisper through the crack between the wall and our bunk bed, "Dominique, we should tell the truth. I don't want to get in trouble."

"Sade', you better not say anything. Ashley is going to beat you up if you snitch. Ma is not going to beat you. She'll hit me, and I'll cry before she can get to you. Just don't say nothing.", I'd whisper back.

Returning with a belt in her hand, Phyllis would make her last attempt for the truth. "Sade, I know you know where Ashley is. Do you want to get a spanking?"

Interjecting before Sade' could answer, I'd stand up so my mother could switch her gaze from Sade' to me. "Ma, you can hit us, but we're not going to say anything because we don't know anything."

At this point, Phyllis was fed up and knew we were lying. Nothing about my little speech was convincing. As promised, I took the first few hits while Sade' cried as if she could feel the pain not being afflicted on her skin. When my mother was done with me, she headed towards Sade'. Through my tears, I'd yell, "I promise, we don't know."

As Phyllis raised her belt, Sade' caved. "Ma, we don't know where she went. When she left out, she told us not to lock the backdoor. I'm sorry for lying. We didn't mean to. We just don't want to get in trouble with Ashley."

This became a reoccurring event in our home. Ashley left the house at night, praying to be back home before my mother. Ashley got caught, one way or another. I lied for Ashley. Sade' tried until she saw my mother's belt, then caved.

Phyllis would express her frustration and fears about Ashley sneaking out and being "only God knows where". But Phyllis did it the only way she knew how; she fussed, and she hit. She figured she could whip Ashley into respecting her boundaries and rules.

Unfortunately, her plan wasn't successful because Phyllis didn't shift her behavior, nor did Ashley. While Phyllis continued to spend time away from the house, so did Ashley. My mother would spend hours yelling at Ashley about the dangers of being out in the streets and leaving us in the house alone. If Sade' and I were in the same space when Phyllis' hurricane of rage let loose, we were getting some of it too.

Phyllis was so fed up with Ashley that Sade' and I felt like she was fed up with us as well. If Sade' or I got in trouble for anything, she'd yell or beat us, then turn around and start on Ashley. It became, if one was in trouble, we all were in trouble. I desperately wanted Nekisha back in the house. But Nekisha had a child of her own and was figuring out adulthood for herself.

A year later, Ashley joined her as she became a teenage mother. Unfortunately, my mother's rigid discipline did not whip Ashley into shape. However, the undesired blessing of a pregnancy was her saving grace.

Phyllis cried many nights, praying her nightmare of Ashley's murder or incarceration would never come true. But what she didn't pray for, and didn't suspect, was a teenage pregnancy. Phyllis was successful in her pursuits with Nekisha. Her oldest child earned her high school diploma and started in the workforce before becoming a mother.

Conversely, Phyllis was not feeling too successful with her second child. While she was doing better in her ability to provide for us, Phyllis was losing control of her second goal; raising us up right. She was angry. But, not just at Ashley. Phyllis was mad at all of us.

With her head high and chest up, she didn't let anyone see her sweat. To the public, Phyllis stood by her daughter 100%. Phyllis told Ashley that she didn't have time to feel sorry for herself. Her childhood life, as she knew it, was over. Phyllis was going to make sure Ashley completed high school. This was not the end for Ashley but a bumpy obstacle to her beginning.

Phyllis didn't speak much about her disappointment after her initial blow up, but we felt it. Her fury towards Ashley's situation clearly spilled over to how she dealt with Sade' and me. If I'm honest, we saw a difference in how she treated me. It's still a mystery how Sade' was often left out of the fiery rage that came my way.

Sade', much like Nekisha, had a unique but complex relationship with our mother. They were buddies. Although Phyllis said she was not interested in being her daughters' friend, Sade' definitely said, "My mother is like my best friend. I can talk to her about anything."

This was not my story. True enough, I understood why Ashley made my mother so upset. But I couldn't, for the life of me, understand what it was about me that made Phyllis so angry. I guess I took up for Ashley, lied for Ashley, and corrected my mother's statements more than I should have. But I couldn't help it. I had a thing for knowledge and truth – except when I was under my sisters' ride-or-die code of conduct.

Additionally, I became sarcastic when I was angry. I was stubborn and stood by my beliefs, and I didn't care if I got a beating because of it. Also, I was often told that I wouldn't just let Phyllis be mad. I made her angrier when I questioned her. But, to my defense, I was getting mixed signals.

Phyllis told us, "Don't try to be like someone else. Be yourself. Be a leader. Don't be naïve and let people tell you anything. Use your common sense."

Phyllis taught us some profound things. I followed what she taught us to the T, and I reminded her that she taught me my ways of being. It was clear that she didn't like when those lessons challenged her supremacy. If it didn't make sense, I questioned it. Then, she fussed and beat me. It was a cycle that I wasn't aware of at the time. Eventually, I stopped trying to figure it out. However, my feelings towards my mother were changing, and my narrative was finding its shape.

When we speak, we are afraid our words will not be heard or welcomed. But when we are silent, we are still afraid. So, it is better to speak.

AUDRE LORDE

Chapter Five:

Children Have Things to Say

Dom Skinner

Let's Talk

Months after Ashley had given birth to her son, Phyllis moved us across town, to the other side of southeast DC. We moved into a newly developed four-bedroom duplex, in the Stanton Glenn Apartment complex. This neighborhood had been completely renovated, and the apartments were sparkling new. However, the people and culture weren't much different from the projects we'd just moved from.

I honestly didn't care. I was excited to finally have my own bedroom and a dishwasher. My bedroom was downstairs next to Ashley's, while Sade's room was upstairs, across from our mother's. It felt like the perfect setup.

During this time, Phyllis was working hard to manage her disappointment. Still, it showed up in the way she spoke to Ashley or about her. Because it's in Phyllis' nature to provide, she didn't allow Ashley to feel like she had to figure it out independently.

Phyllis still cared about how people viewed her. She worked hard to make sure we didn't make the same choices she'd made. Phyllis needed us to be her redeeming points because we were a reflection of her. As a result, she made sure Ashley had everything she needed to finish high school. Yet, in the process, she made herself very clear, "I will not be raising your child. I am here to support you. But you will figure it out."

The way Phyllis began speaking to Ashley spilled over to how she communicated with me and Sade'. She didn't filter her words. Whatever she thought, she said. Phyllis began to lack patience altogether. She had a short fuse and was ready to blow at any minute. While my sisters learned to get used to this behavior, I did not. They'd say, "Well, you know how she is." every time I complained about her hitting me or yelling at me.

I remembered Nekisha telling me, "If you stop talking back to her, she will stop hitting you."

Dom Skinner

I told her, "If I breathe wrong, ma will hit me and tell me to get it together."

My sister laughed and said I was exaggerating. I admit I was not an "I'll take what you do to me" type of child. I asked questions like, "why are you yelling?" or "why does that make you so angry?". I also didn't like my mother to place her assumptions on me.

Phyllis had a way of telling us about ourselves. I never liked people making things up about me that weren't true, and I especially hated it with Phyllis. I'd say, "that's not true."

My sisters would tell me, "Dominique, just shut up. Let her talk."

I'd respond with, "But that's not true. It's a lie."

All Phyllis heard was 'I called her a liar'. Then, there was a slap across my face. Events like this would happen like a broken record on repeat. I didn't like her making assumptions about me, and she didn't like me correcting her, especially in front of other people.

Then, Phyllis began saying, "I don't want to hear what you have to say. I know you."

In my hurt, I'd respond, "You don't know me."

Phyllis' last rebuttal was always, "I know you because I had you."

As a result of these inevitable arguments and beatings, I hated being in the house when Phyllis was home. So, when I saw the signup sheet for track and field while walking through the halls of my new school, I didn't hesitate to sign up. I knew Phyllis would allow me to join. If nothing else, my mother wanted to make sure we did not have idle time. She hated that

80

Sade' and I kept asking to visit our friends from our old neighborhood.

Before moving, the community was getting worse due to the community centers closing. A few of our friends had been shot or arrested. Phyllis also wanted to prevent us from following down the same path as Ashley. As I thought, Phyllis signed those papers with quickness. The day I signed up to run track for Johnson Junior High School, my life was forever changed.

My eighth-grade year quickly turned into one of the best years of my childhood. I joined the track team and never looked back. The team was fresh. The coaches were new to the school, and most of the girls were new to the sport. Our coaches were Coach Cherry and Coach Perry, two guys that went above and beyond to create a dynamic team. With a group of eight girls, we were winning the DCIAA championships. We were unstoppable.

Most importantly, we were like family. We fought often and argued about everything and nothing substantial. But, when it was time to compete, we were each other's biggest fans. Our relay teams were solid. I will admit that I didn't like to train, but I rarely missed a practice. If anything, I wanted to be where I felt understood.

During our indoor season, I was the first leg of our 4x200 relay team. I was sprinting in to complete the handoff, and my teammate didn't take off like we'd practiced. I tried not to run her down with my spikes, so I stepped off the track after making sure the baton was secured in her hand. I tripped over a beam and hurt my foot. I was happy that I didn't have to run the open 400-meter race because I was tired. But, while I was sitting there with the bag of ice on my foot, the pain wouldn't go away.

Luckily, Phyllis always tried to make her way to my track meets. She couldn't take staying throughout the entire meet, but she would make sure she saw me run at least one of my races. It was typically towards the end, so she could take me home. But this meet, Phyllis happened to be there for most of the event.

When the team was gearing up for the last event, the 4x400 meter relay, everyone was looking at me like, "you better be okay to run this race." Phyllis was on the side of my teammates.

I told them there was no way I was able to run. I didn't think I could walk because it was so painful. When Coach Cherry took my ice pack off, my foot had swollen double in size. When Phyllis took me to the emergency room, they informed us that there were a few torn tissues, and I needed to stay off my foot for it to heal.

I was on crutches for a few weeks. Although I couldn't train, I went to practice every day. While the team was doing their warmups and drills, I was spending time with the coaches. We would talk about the track events and compare times of other teams. They let me watch some of the tapes from our previous track meets to study my performance and my competition.

Of the two, I spent most of my time with Coach Perry. He was really easy to talk to. I never felt the need to appear put together around him, like I did with my teachers. I often hid the trauma I was experiencing in my house. Sometimes I made up stories about how awesome things were in my home. Not because anyone asked or cared. I think I desperately needed to escape my own thoughts.

But eventually, I slowly began opening up to Coach Perry. He was the first person to just listen to me without making me feel like an ungrateful child. Whenever I would complain about my mother, my family would remind me that I only get one mother and I should be lucky to have her. I felt like my pain fell on deaf ears, so I became silent, which only made me resent my mother even more. But Coach was different. He didn't judge my mother or me. He just listened and asked, "Are you okay?"

I remember when I was around seven years old, I'd gotten hurt and needed to go to the emergency room. While sitting in the waiting room, Phyllis looked at me and said, "you've got to be more careful. These people are going to start thinking I'm abusing you, and they will take you from me. Do you want to be like some of your friends who are in foster care?"

I also cried at the thought of being taken away from my mother. I knew a few people who lived in foster care or with extended family members because their parents were on drugs. Their lives seemed more challenging than I could have ever imagined. While I dealt with some painful things in my house, I knew my life was filled with privileges that kids in my communities only dreamed of.

Though I desired to feel seen and loved, I wasn't going to risk the stability Phyllis provided by sharing all the details of her shortcomings. So, I always ended our talks with, "yeah, I'm fine. I just get tired of her yelling all the time."

While I was still ineligible to run, Coach would always drop me off at home after practice. Sometimes, if we ended practice early, he'd ask if I wanted to ride with him to see his wife, Krissi. He knew how much I loved his wife. I always wondered about her. So, I'd get excited to make the quick drive to take her food. We spent that time talking about everything.

When my foot healed, and I returned to practice, we continued our ritual of watching race film, and Coach driving me home. The crime around the school started to get worse, so he'd offer to take more of the team home. Between him and Coach Cherry, all of us were getting rides home. Although I lived the closest to the school, I would ask if I could ride to drop everyone off before he took me home. He never asked why. He just said, "Sure, that's fine with me." I think he knew why, but he never brought it up.

Once the season started to slow down, Coach Perry asked me if I'd like to help his wife, Krissi, at her salon for a few hours after practice. But only on the days we ended early, which were Wednesdays and Fridays. My dreams were coming true. I was going to be able to spend less time at home.

I wasn't sure what my mother was going to say. As much as Phyllis respected my coaches and their wives, she still didn't trust men around her daughters. Because of her past, she kept a close eye on every man that was near us. But, to my surprise, Phyllis gave her consent, and I started spending more of my evenings with the Perrys. This was the beginning of me being adopted into their family.

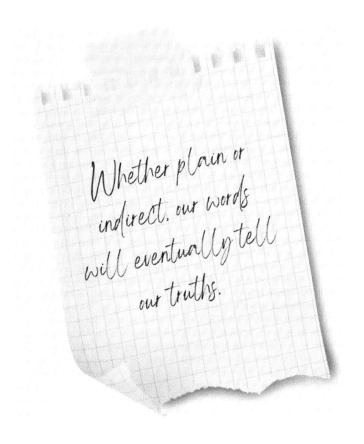

Whether plain or indirect, our words will eventually tell our truths.

My Blended Family

Over time, I spent more and more time away from my house. Between school, track practice, and track meet, my schedule was already tight. I was also spending a few evenings a week, and Saturdays, at Krissi's salon. Then, my godbrother, Lil Steve, started coming around again. He'd pick me up and take me wherever I wanted to go. We spent most of the time at the movies, though. I was pressed to see the latest movies.

Steve wanted to make sure I stayed connected to the family, so he'd take me to the family events or hang out with a few of the cousins. I was still feeling like an outsider, but at least this time, my brother was walking me through it. Outside of family time, Lil Steve wanted to make sure he was the one to teach me how to drive. That's what big brothers are for. Right? Of course, he wasn't going to wait until I was old enough to apply for a driver's permit because there was no better time than the present.

When it was late, and the traffic was slow, Steve would say, "You ready to drive?"

I never back down from an adventure, so my answer was always, "Yep!"

This was supposed to be a secret because there was no way Phyllis was going to be okay with her 13-year-old daughter driving. Because Phyllis is a detective, or I was too loud when telling Sade' the details of how great I am at driving, the secret was out of the bag, and Lil Steve was in trouble. She let him have it. He was used to my mother going off about one thing or another, so he didn't react to her harsh words.

But Phyllis wasn't going to let it go that easily. She called my godfather, Steve, and snitched on us. We didn't get in as much trouble as we thought. I think Big Steve was just happy that we were building our relationship as siblings.

Out of respect for my mother and not wanting to lose his privilege of picking me up, Lil Steve told Phyllis that he wouldn't allow me to drive again. After a few weeks, I was begging him to let me behind the wheel. We had to create a brother-sister secrecy so that I wouldn't talk about driving unless I was driving. Of course, I said whatever he wanted me to say. I was just itching to drive. I clearly spoke about it to my friends.

When I wasn't hanging out with my brother, I spent extra time with the Perrys. If they asked me if I wanted to come over or go someplace with them, my answer was always "yes." My mother seemed to be home more than she ever was when I was a younger child.

However, our relationship had become toxic. It was challenging to be around Phyllis for long periods of time without her lashing out at me or me sarcastically responding to her. So, I avoided her as much as I could, but it wasn't always possible because she was also showing up more than she ever had before. But now I didn't want her to.

Phyllis showed up for almost every one of my track meets, even when we were traveling. My coaches and teammates loved it. She was often the only parent there to support the team, and she never came empty-handed. She brought snacks, fruit, water, and Gatorade for everyone. She was the loudest person in the stands, cheering on everyone on my team. The team thought she was the best. I think I was the only person not excited for her to be around.

Yet, I would become extremely pissed off if she couldn't make it to a meet. Part of me believed she didn't make it because I wasn't significant to her. While another part of me thought she only came around to brag about all the things she did for me.

My relationship with her was so unstable that I couldn't be happy around her but felt terrible if she didn't show up. I believe the Perrys sensed it. They weren't sure what was going on in my relationship with my mother, and they never officially asked. They just started filling me up with unconditional love.

One Saturday, Krissi and I were finishing up a long day at the hair salon. I was sweeping up the freshly cut hair from the floor while Krissi was curling her last client's hair. Routinely, she asked if I was hungry, and I said "yes."

Without missing a beat or looking up from the women's hair, she said, "Call your father and ask him if he wants us to pick up some fried fish before going home."

I said, "Okay!" thinking she meant to say "coach."

Then the woman in the chair said, "Krissi, what grade is your daughter in?"

She responded, "She's going to the ninth grade next year."

As the phone rang in my ear, I thought, "Oh, she meant what she said."

I wore the biggest smile as I asked "my father" if he wanted us to pick up fried fish. From that moment on, Krissi told the world I was her daughter.

She began introducing me to the family, saying, "This is your cousin Margo. This is your Pop-Pop and Grandma Lucy. This is your Uncle Shawn.", and the list goes on. But it wasn't one-sided because Coach Perry started doing the same thing.

While I wasn't legally adopted until years later, at that moment, Vaughn and Krissi Perry became my additional parents. There wasn't a discussion, and no one asked any questions. Or at least not around me. Everyone just accepted me as Vaughn and Krissi's daughter. Even Vaughn's son, Johari, just said, "Okay." when we met. Was this what it felt like to just be accepted and loved without conditions?

My joy didn't just come from them telling the world that I was their kid. It was the small things that I'd forgotten I needed, like them curling up on the couch with me to watch a movie or us sitting around the table to play board games.

Krissi and I would go shopping and drive around listening to music. We had open and honest conversations about everything. Nothing was off-limits. Except whenever I brought up sports. While we had terrific mother-daughter time, she had a way of making sure I soaked up the love from Vaughn as well. She loved to say, "talk to your dad."

While I was discovering parental affection from my new parents, I was experiencing mixed feelings about Phyllis. But they loved her. There was no doubt that my mother was consistent in her ability to provide the best for my sisters and me. There was nothing she wouldn't buy or pay for, if we asked. That's what she worked so hard to do. Phyllis didn't just give to her daughters. She made offers to her nieces, nephews, and younger cousins. Her giving sometimes extended to our friends.

Many of our friends and even cousins have said, "I wish Phyllis was my mother. She's so cool. She's so open and free with y'all, and she buys y'all everything."

Anytime Phyllis felt we were unruly or ungrateful, she'd remind us that people wish they had a mother like her. To be honest, our lives were very different from some of our cousins and friends. We were well-traveled, well dressed, and well mannered. We were not rich, but Phyllis made sure we didn't appear poor. No matter how much she cursed and fussed in our home, she expected us to show up like we had sense, as she would say.

Overall, Phyllis demanded our best and nothing less. She reminded us often that she'd give us the piece of the world that she could grab, if we did our part. And she did, time after time. Even if she reminded us of it the entire time or fussed at us as she checked out at the cash register. This, however, was my worst nightmare. I despised nothing more than my mother fussing in public, but it never stopped her.

For instance, while shopping for clothes, which I didn't want to do on this particular day, Phyllis picked up everything she thought I needed to add to my wardrobe. As the cashier started scanning the items and the total price started to add up, a woman in line made jokes about how my mother just bought us a whole wardrobe. Phyllis thrives on communicating with strangers. So, naturally, they began talking about raising teenagers.

Then she began commenting, "I shouldn't be spending this type of money when they don't even do what I ask, and if they do, they take their precious time."

As she and the lady were going on and on, I began taking items off the counter and said, "I'll put these back. I don't want any of it."

She snatched the things from my hand and yelled even more. I couldn't take it. I made the mistake of trying to walk away. Phyllis hit me in front of everyone in the line. While I fought back the tears from being beyond embarrassed, I heard the woman say, "She deserved that." I wanted to scream but knew it would only make the situation worse.

While it was embarrassing and I hated going shopping with her, I appreciated every item I asked for and all the extra stuff that I didn't. I never had to worry about how I would be able to participate in an activity or sport. Between Phyllis, my godfather, Steve, and Delvon, there wasn't an item I couldn't get access to or a place I couldn't go.

Because I was an honor student and a thriving athlete, they ensured I had everything I asked for. Between my achievements and Phyllis' track record of provision, everyone praised her for being a wonderful mother. Even my adopted parents, Vaughn and Krissi, gave her praise. If I'm honest, it confused me. They'd witnessed me in some of my darkest times, but they admired her.

Obviously, there was something I wasn't seeing. Maybe I was an ungrateful child.

When we spend more time focusing on what's lacking, we fail to appreciate our blessings.

Chapter Six:

Let It Go

Dom Skinner

My Sweet Life

Throughout my high school years, my focus shifted completely. I was no longer consumed with my feelings around my parents. I was in a place of acceptance; Checko was living his life in Jamaica, and Phyllis was working to do both their parts. I even accepted that my mother was supportive in all my endeavors.

She showed up to every track meet, most award programs, and even a presentation if she knew about it. In addition, I accepted that she would show up loud, possibly frustrated by my frustration of her being abrasive, and our collective frustration was going to lead to her talking at me for hours about her many sacrifices. I just accepted all of it.

When I was in high school, my relationship with Phyllis had more ups than downs. As I'm writing this book, I realized how much I'd detached myself from my childhood desires. I was no longer crying about my mother's behavior towards me.

Also, I finally took my sisters' advice; I stopped talking. Now, I didn't stop talking entirely because that would go against who I am as a person, which is Phyllis' daughter. We are some talking people. However, I became passive in my relationship with her. I viewed our relationship as transactional. If I did this, she provided that. That's all she talked about, and that's what folks praised her on.

I got to the point where I viewed my situation as the sweetest life any teenager could have. No one around me had what I had. When I recognized that, I had to tell myself, "Yo, you have it sweet."

I had adopted parents who loved me without conditions, I could be freely me, and they accepted all of me. I basically had two homes with two different atmospheres. My parents, Vaughn and Krissi, were my emotional support. They didn't have to provide for me financially because Phyllis had that on lock. But that didn't stop them from giving me gifts and providing experiences.

Then, I had my godfather, Steve, whose favorite question was, "What do you need?" While he wasn't showing up for track meets or award ceremonies, or even spending time with me, he didn't mind covering the bill for all my miscellaneous wants. Phyllis, and the Perrys, were strategic in what they bought me. If they thought it was a waste of money, the answer was "No." But, not with Steve.

One day I had a random thought, "It would be really cool to have a video camera."

The thought ended there. I had no idea what I would do with it, and no part of my imagination convinced me that I was a filmmaker. But that didn't stop me from making a call to my "dad."

"Hey, daddy! How are you? So, you know I got straight A's again this term, right? I was thinking, is it possible for you to buy me a video camera?" Of course, he asked why I wanted a video camera, and of course, I made up something on the spot.

A few weeks later, I was walking through Radio Shack to pick out my new toy. I had no clue what I was looking for, but I was a happy camper. The sales clerk showed me a few different models before asking, "So, what features are most important to you?"

I told him, "I just want to be able to record stuff at school."

He got excited at the thought of me being part of my school's film department. I told him the truth, "I go to H.D Woodson. I don't even think we have a film department. I just want to record me and my friends so we can remember these moments."

Let's Talk

After spending an hour in Radio Shack, I walked out with my brand-new Sony handheld video camera. I used that thing for the first few weeks, then it stayed in my closet for months. Every time I asked for something new, Phyllis would refer to the video camera she hadn't seen since I brought it to her house. Which meant she wasn't going to buy what I wasn't going to use.

To be fair, I took the video camera on my senior trip, and I have some fantastic footage. By fantastic, I mean hilarious moments of great jokes and laughter, but the video is pointing at the ground because my video skills were terrible.

Thankfully, Steve never followed up with the story I told him. He probably knew I made it up. Sometimes, he'd ask how the video camera was working out. But, other than that, we were good. Between him, Lil Steve, and Delvon, I was living the best teenage life. I always had the funds to hang out with my friends. Both of my mothers, Phyllis and Krissi, love to shop, so my wardrobe was full. To top it all off, I had older sisters who let me drive their cars or didn't kill me when I took them without asking.

My high school life was so sweet that my blessings often spilled over to my friends and teammates. My best friends, Monique, Brittany, Sada, and I, lived the high school dream. My sister, Ashley, would take us to the Go-Go and keep it a secret. Our classmates couldn't wait to hear about our weekend adventures on Monday mornings. Also, Phyllis loved our friendship, so when I asked for money to "be with the girls," she never questioned it.

At some point, she stopped asking where we were going. Because I was an honor student and athlete, Phyllis never yelled at me about my whereabouts. She trusted that I was responsible. Actually, this is how all of my parents viewed me.

If I'm honest, I wasn't the good teenager they thought I was. The truth is, I have the best sisters in the world. Ashley covered for me more time than I could think. She would joke about how much I got in trouble for other things, so she didn't want Phyllis to beat me up for exploring as a teenager.

But Ashley wasn't reckless in her pursuits of me having fun. She, secretly, thought I was lame because I was different from the rest of them. For instance, I read books for enjoyment, I wanted to discuss random historical facts and which songs referenced said facts, etc. So, she also wasn't too worried.

Ashley had lived through some crazy experiences and survived most of them. She didn't send me out into the world without knowledge. Ashley made sure that I was street savvy with a keen sense of awareness. The way I moved was as if I was pushing weight like Jay-Z before he released the Reasonable Doubt album. In other words, I paid close attention to how people moved around me, and what was being said. I never indulged in too much fun because I was taught to keep my eyes open and my head on a swivel.

Ashley would tell her friends, "I can't have my baby sister out here with just her book smarts. She has to be intelligent all the way around."

~~~

Side note: *Ashley gave me my foundation for school and the world. So, shout out to big sisters who unknowingly make way for their baby sisters to be great!*

~~~

My friends and I were genius at getting over on our parents. I had the nerve to have two homes. Because everything was so sweet, I had no plans on messing it up by getting on Phyllis' bad side. I just accepted that she was still who she was. Phyllis still had a way of adding a few hurtful comments when she was frustrated. But I'd become numb to it. So, I let it roll off my back like water off a duck.

My eyes would shut tight, and I'd take a deep exhale before saying, "Ma, you got it." In order words, I refused to argue.

However, I often allowed her words to linger, which resulted in me being passive-aggressive towards her. At times, she'd feel it and, without warning, she would slap me across my face. During this time of our relationship, I was numb to her hits as well. So, the tears were no longer welling up in my eyes. But rage was boiling under my skin.

"Walk away, Dominique. It's not worth it."

This became my regular self-talk.

It's important to take inventory of our actions. especially when we feel righteous in our behavior towards those who've hurt us.

A Different Relationship

August 2007, I rolled up to Winston-Salem State University, ready to conquer my college experience. Between my gang of parents and my extended family, I had everything I needed and more for me and Brittany's dorm room. The most important thing was, I had a trunk full of hair supplies and tools.

My mother, Krissi, said there was no way I would be away from home with my hair looking crazy. She and Phyllis tag teamed on getting me every item I needed, from curling rods to a hot comb, to hair relaxers and treatments. Everything Krissi had in her hair salon, I had in my hair trunk for school.

Phyllis and my sisters went to Costco and racked up all the snacks, dorm food, vitamins, and toiletries. Sade' was the first one in our house to go away to college. The year before I made my entrance at WSSU, Phyllis dropped Sade' off in Raleigh, NC, at Shaw University. That was Phyllis' first introduction to what students needed while they're away from home.

My sister, Sade', was quite particular. For lack of better words, she was extra. So, everything Phyllis brought her to make sure she was comfortable at school, she got for me. Now, I'm not complaining because that just meant there was more to share with Brittany, and our friends Ashley Jo and ReDonah, who'd also gone to H.D Woodson with us.

When Phyllis gave me her final hug before getting back on the road to DC, she cried. It was awkward. Not her crying because she did that often. But the long hug and tears combination was a little weird.

A few days before my departure from DC, she and I had a disagreement about something. Later that day, I overheard her on the phone saying that she was sick and tired of me and couldn't wait for me to be gone.

I added this to my internal archive that supported my belief, "Phyllis hates me." So, I couldn't view the hug nor the tears as genuine. I thought to myself, "She would have been a great actress. Let me go along with the show."

Once we were settled in our dorm room, Brittany commented on how Phyllis went all out.

I said, "Oh, girl, it's just so she can brag to her friends about all the things she bought. It's for her to look good. She'll call me complaining about it tomorrow."

As I'm laughing at my comment, Brittany said, "Well, I'm happy she hooked us up."

As I expected, Phyllis was ringing my room phone at 7:30am. In my true "stop bothering me" fashion, I ignored the call. She called back, then she called my cell phone.

Brittany yelled across the room, "Girl, answer the phone. Phyllis is going to keep calling."

I answered the phone because I felt that Brittany was a few seconds from throwing her pillow at me. To my surprise, Phyllis was chipper and full of energy. Phyllis was asking me questions like we were long-time girlfriends who hadn't talked in a while.

She said, "So, catch me up. How was the freshman event last night? Did you show Brittany where we put the snacks? Did you sleep well on that mattress? I know it's nothing like your mattress here."

The questions were coming a mile a minute. Again, I was confused. I almost asked her who was around her. Instead, I just answered the questions.

She ended the call with, "Alright, I'm going to let you go because you don't seem like you want to talk. Oh, and don't forget to stretch and take your vitamins."

Dom Skinner

This became her energy while I was away at school. Brittany would always joke about how much Phyllis missed me when I was away but was ready for me to leave when I was near her. While Brittany was joking, it was true. To some degree, the feeling was mutual.

I spent two years at Winston- Salem State University. But I visited home at least once a month to attend my orthodontics appointments, which also gave me an excuse to see my boyfriend, at the time. During the summer before my sophomore year, I'd talked to each of my parents about getting me a car. Everyone said, "No." Phyllis was adamant about telling everyone why I didn't need a car.

"She just wants to be up and down the i95 highway, every chance she gets. She needs to stay down in North Carolina."

Everyone agreed with her. True enough she was right. I was already hopping in anybody's car who told me they were going to the DC area for the weekend. I'd kick them some gas money and have my bag packed ready for our five-hour drive back to DC for a 48-hour visit.

As much as I loved traveling home once a month for a weekend, my heart broke when I didn't get housing for my junior year. Winston-Salem State University thought it was a great idea to put the students in a lottery to determine if they'd receive a dorm assignment. The semesters prior, seniority and GPA determined your ranking to choose campus housing.

I was excited. I was an upcoming junior, and I was on the Dean's List. I knew I was going to be amongst the first to pick my dorm. I already had in my mind that I would choose a single room in Rams Common Hall. But the day we received that email informing us about the lottery, something in my spirit said, "you're out of luck on having your own room."

Unfortunately, I wasn't assigned housing at all. I tried convincing my parents that I needed a car to stay in Winston-

100

Salem because the public transportation system was not as reliable as Metro in DC. I was cool with moving off campus. Brittany was happy with her off-campus housing, I figured I would be too. But I wasn't going to do it without a vehicle.

The parents didn't budge. I felt like I'd lost my gift of "getting what I wanted." As a result, I transferred my records to Bowie State University in Bowie, Maryland. I was officially leaving WSSU.

A week before finals, I randomly checked my student account. My eyes lit up when my report revealed that I had a pending refund of over $11,000. This couldn't have been true because I'd already received a $1,500 refund a month after the semester had started. I also didn't get any notifications for additional scholarships.

I thought to myself, "Financial Aid done messed around and put someone's money in my account. Let me go clear this up."

My boyfriend tried to convince me to stay quiet about it. As much as I wanted to purchase a car and get an apartment off campus, it didn't feel right to keep what didn't belong to me.

The woman in the Financial Aid office was lovely. It was clear that the semester was ending because the office was empty, and the staff was patient. Which is the complete opposite of the first few weeks of each semester.

There is typically an influx of students waiting in line to determine why their classes were purged from their schedules. But on that day, the woman had time to listen to my jokes about accidentally stealing someone's refund check.

She did a quick check on her computer then in her binder before saying, "Sweetie, that's your money."

I said, "No, ma'am. It is not. I know every scholarship and grant I received this semester, and I already received my refund check months ago. I don't want to take this check, and y'all call me asking for y'all money back."

She laughed at me and said, "Girl, if you don't sign for this check so I can take my break."

I signed for the check, and I walked away like I was hiding the secret recipe for Coca-Cola. I put the check in a purse that I'd already packed up. I had to keep it safe because I knew that same woman would email me to inform me that it was a mistake.

I told my parents about it, and each of them said, "Look, now you can buy your own car."

But I was scared. I told them that I wasn't going to deposit the check until I was sure. They agreed that was a smart decision. My boyfriend, on the other hand, thought I was crazy.

After my last final, I packed up all my things and headed back to Washington, DC, for good this time. When I got home, Phyllis told me to give her the check so I wouldn't be tempted to spend it. I reassured her that I did not want to owe WSSU that money back. However, I did as I was instructed, knowing I could trust her to keep me honest. I watched her put it in her Bible.

She said, "God will tell you what to do with it."

Something about Phyllis was looking lighter. She was less frustrated and angry. She wasn't throwing life lessons and parables at me. She was singing and smiling. Most importantly, my silence wasn't bothering her. Phyllis was in her own world.

I figured it was because she basically had an empty house. I was splitting my time between her house and my parents'. Sade' had moved into her own apartment. Nekisha and Ashley were also out of her house, living their adult lives as mothers.

I soon learned, the real reason she was glowing, and seemingly more likable, was because she was dating again.

Phyllis had dated throughout my childhood, but never seriously. It had also been decades since she'd allowed a man to sleep over at her house.

But this was a new chapter of her life, and Phyllis was on cloud nine. She was showing up as a different person. Honestly, I was excited for her. My sisters and I often joked about how much we wanted her to get a man. We figured if she was in a relationship, she'd lighten up a bit. And it appeared that we were correct.

When I met her guy, he seemed okay. I didn't like, nor dislike, him. But we didn't really talk much. However, I asked him questions about his intentions with my mother. I tried to do the thing I saw kids do on TV shows. I didn't really care, though.

It was just good to see her smiling. She was acting like a teenager with a crush. Whenever she picked me up from my parents' house, she always wanted to talk about him, the things he liked, or their conversations. She was so smitten by him that I was witnessing a different version of her, that I'd never seen before.

Phyllis even offered to pick up my boyfriend and asked if he'd like to stay the night when it became too late for him to catch his train home. This was totally out of the ordinary from the Phyllis we knew. Of course, she asked him to help me clean her house. That was a requirement for anyone who came over.

Keeping her home clean and tidy was unnegotiable. We were taught that our Saturday mornings were dedicated to "top to bottom" cleaning, windows and walls were included. Growing up, Phyllis always made her way home on Saturday morning for her call and response routine.

~~~

Phyllis: "God is good."

Dom Skinner

Everyone in her house: "All the time."

Phyllis: "And all the time."

Everyone: "God is good."

~~~

She'd follow up with a praise song that she was creating in that moment. When Phyllis noticed that we weren't out of our beds, she'd begin banging on walls and opening doors, saying, "Get up and clean my house. It's already after 8 o'clock. I bet y'all think y'all got plans today. Nobody's going anywhere, and don't ask me for anything until my house is clean."

Phyllis was consistent. So, I'd already prepped the boyfriend, and he was ready to say, "No problem, Ms. Phyllis." The plan was to stay on her good side.

After being back in DC for two months and not receiving an email from Winston-Salem State University about the mysterious refund check, my parents and I figured it was a good time to start looking for a car. Between Phyllis, Krissi, and Vaughn, I visited so many car dealerships. I dedicated hours to looking at vehicles on the internet and spent countless hours daydreaming about the car I would call mine. It would have black leather seats, a sunroof, tinted windows, and a navigation system.

To my surprise, $11,000 was not a lot of money. More importantly, I couldn't afford what I was dreaming of, especially since my only job was working part time as my mother, Krissi's, shampoo assistant. Nonetheless, I finally found a vehicle within my budget that I actually liked. It was a used 2007 Chrysler Sebring, with moderate mileage on it.

It was nothing like I'd envisioned. It had none of the sparkling features. The seats were light gray and cloth, and the features were as basic as car features can get. Except, I had power windows and a port for an Aux cord. At least I could plug in my Sony MP3 player.

After looking at it online for a few days, I started to appreciate the asking price and began picturing myself rolling through the city. After showing all my parents, they thought it was a good fit and price. Phyllis offered to take me to the dealership to do the negotiation.

She said, "I don't want them to up the price on you. You look like an easy target."

My dad, Vaughn, agreed that I would have a better deal if Phyllis put her spin on it. He was right. They dropped the price by $1,000, and my interest rate was at 2%. At 19 years old, I brought my first car, with a car payment of $136/ month. Meanwhile, I still don't know where that money came from.

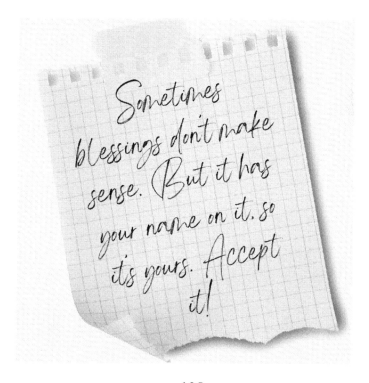

Our Darkest Days

The summer before my first semester at Bowie State University was blissful. I finally had my own car, and I was coming and going as I pleased. Thankfully, I didn't have a curfew at either of my homes. All the parents wanted to know was if I was safe and when I got to my destination.

My boyfriend and I were exploring the city and spending weekends at the beach. I was present at almost every cookout, game night, and party. I was picking people up and dropping folks off. I was feeling generous and free while having a fantastic time.

Additionally, Phyllis and I were stable in our relationship. I was still in the space of acceptance. My mother was who she was, and so was I. Phyllis was still unapologetic in her words, and I was undoubtedly passive-aggressive. This was our accepted norm. When I stayed at her house, we gave each other just enough space to keep the peace. Sometimes, she and I would cook together while listening to music or waiting for my sisters to arrive for dinner.

But when a disagreement developed, I would dismiss myself and head to my parents' house. Phyllis would call and leave long voicemails or text messages to fuss about the altercation. Sometimes, it was right away. Other times, she'd wait until the next day to leave a message with a calmer tone. She often finished her statement with, "It's so sad how disrespectful you are. You won't appreciate me until I'm dead and gone."

This is what I called our stable relationship. Now, as an adult, I realized there were other ways to handle some of our altercations. However, in those moments, I believed the best thing was to leave the environment. I was unaware of how much anger I was holding. But what I did know was that it was my responsibility to leave the space before I screamed out.

Let's Talk

Whenever my mother would begin speaking in a condescending tone, I felt an internal burning rushing through my body. I understood my action as a sign of respect for myself and my mother. I didn't want to be talked at or down to. Respectfully, I didn't want to yell at her. Removing myself was a win for everyone. Eventually, respect lost its value between us.

~~~

Towards the end of the summer, one of my younger cousins asked to move to DC with Phyllis to avoid getting in trouble in Tarboro, NC. During this time, Phyllis was happy that she no longer had children in her house. As much as she wanted to say "no," it wasn't sitting well in her spirit. So naturally, Phyllis looked for validations to support her reasoning.

With Jay-Z's American Gangster album blasting through my laptop speakers, I could still hear Phyllis' voice as she discussed the situation with the person on the other end of her cellphone.

"Why does she have to take all of her calls on speakerphone?" I said to myself as I closed my bedroom door.

Midway through my jam, 'No Hook,' I heard my door open. "Damn, I knew I should have left the door open. She's about to go off", I thought as I turned to face her.

But to my surprise, she wanted to share the details of her conversation. I turned down the volume as Phyllis stood in my doorway going on about what this person and that person said. I'd grown accustomed to holding in my thoughts unless I heard a question, and it was directed to me. So, I continued organizing my clothes as she spoke.

"Dominique! Did you hear what I said?" Phyllis said in an exacerbated tone.

"I'm listening.", I responded while finally hitting the pause button on my laptop screen.

107

"So, what do you think?"

"Let him come.",

"I knew you were going to say that. I'm tired of taking care of children. Why is it that everyone always wants to come live with me?" Phyllis went on as she paced in the hall near my bedroom.

I pressed play and returned to my clothes without saying anything else. About two songs later, my mother stood in my doorway again and said, "Why did you say to let him come?"

At this point, I was annoyed that my jam session was being interrupted. Listening to one of Jay-Z's albums from start to finish was a daily ritual. As I listened to the albums, I organized, I colored, I cleaned, I imagined. This was my time of freedom to escape my world and dedicate my imagination to my favorite people that I hadn't met yet. So, I took a deep breath and pressed pause again.

"Because that's what you want to do."

Right after this slid out of my mouth, I knew I should have said something else.

"Who told you I wanted another child in my house? Don't y'all know I'm tired of children? See, y'all don't know me at all.", she fussed. The "y'all" Phyllis referred to are my sisters and me.

I finally shared that the school system in Washington, DC had more opportunities than Tarboro, NC and that she had the extra space. At the time, my younger cousin was grieving his mother's death and needed to be in a new environment. Plus, my sisters and I were willing to help in this transition.

As I suspected, Phyllis agreed and became a guardian of a teenager again. She asked me to be around more to help her, and

I said, "sure." The following week, my cousin, Q, was fully moved in.

As promised, I stepped into the big cousin role and was available whenever I was needed. Having my own car was most definitely a huge help. Q was adjusting to the new space and school, and it seemed to be going well. He was finding his way by exploring new friendships, sports, and the city.

Meanwhile, Phyllis was exploring new territory as well. Up until that point, Phyllis had never merged her dating life and parenting life. They had been exclusively separate since she and Steve parted ways in the early 1990s. However, in this new season, Phyllis was allowing herself to flow freely in love. My sisters and I were excited about what was possible when she put focus on her own happiness. Yet, the expected harmony gradually turned into our darkest days.

During the Back-to-School night at Q's school, I told my mother that I would meet them after my last class at BSU. I figured if I was going to help, the least I could do was start by making sure his paperwork was successfully transferred.

By the time I was in high school, I was handling all my school paperwork and only took it to Phyllis for her signature. Sometimes she'd grant me permission to sign for her if her schedule didn't allow her to be present. My mother hadn't dealt with school paperwork in years. The last thing we needed was for her to be frustrated to the point of sending him back to Tarboro.

I pulled up to the school, ready with my list of questions. As a person barely twenty years old, I took myself way too seriously. After a few calls and text messages, I finally met up with Q, my mother, and her boyfriend. Together, we went from class to class, meeting teachers and learning about upcoming programs. As we were making our way up the stairs to the last location, I heard Phyllis say, "What are you looking at?"

"No! No! No! This is not happening.", I thought.

Phyllis' boyfriend mumbled something, and my heart started beating out of my chest. Every comment my mother ever made about my body started flooding my mind, and I immediately felt angry. I moved to the side, pretending to tie my shoes to allow them to walk ahead of me.

To avoid my body being a topic of conversation, I made up an excuse and told Q that I needed to get going. I told Phyllis that I'd be staying at Krissi and Vaughn's. When I got to my car, I called my boyfriend to vent my frustration. But he couldn't understand what I was angry about. To be honest, I couldn't articulate the reasons for my emotions either. So, I chose to let it go.

At that point, I'd never told anyone, not even my therapist, how I was shamed by my mother for stretching in the living room after track practice when she walked in the house with a male friend, or the backlash I received while attempting a dance, by the singer Ciara, with my sisters Delvon and his friends walked through the door. There were many stories I never allowed to leave my mind or escape through my words.

While I shared the nasty things my father's girlfriend, Patrice, said about me, I would never allow myself to share how my mother treated me because of my body. As a kid, simply being a kid, my body was often up for discussion.

Phyllis mentioned that she was inappropriately touched, by a friend of the family, when she was a child. While "play" uncles, cousins, and other males were often around, my mother never allowed us to sit on a man's lap or forced us to hug and kiss men as respectful greetings. Because of her experience, she was often wary of letting us sleep over at our friends' houses. But when she did, we had "the talk" when she picked us up.

"Did anyone touch you down there?" She'd say as she pointed between our legs. Phyllis would ask us a series of follow-up questions before she trusted that no one made us feel uncomfortable.

My sisters and I were aware that Phyllis would go to great lengths to protect us from molestation. One of those sacrifices was not allowing her male companions to live with us or stay over. As I mentioned before, I've always had a naturally curvy physique. This was not the case for my mother nor any of my sisters.

I genuinely believe Phyllis was concerned about how men looked at me in a predatory way, and she wanted to protect me from harm. Yet, the way she communicated her concerns left me feeling like I'd done something wrong.

So, when I heard the words, "What are you looking at?" I knew this wasn't good. My sisters and I were just laughing and joking about how Phyllis was about to get her groove back like Angela Bassett in the 1998 film, "How Stella Got Her Groove Back." The last thing I wanted was to be the reason for it not happening. More so, I didn't want to be blamed for someone looking at me.

For most of my life, I loved to be correct. However, this was a time I was praying to be wrong. A few days after Back-to-School night, I decided to stay at my mother's house to avoid the additional twenty minutes it would take to drive to campus from my parents' house.

As I sat in my bed preparing for my exam the following day, Phyllis knocked on the door and asked if I was asleep. When she opened the door, I told her that I was studying for my test. She came in, closed the door behind her, and sat at the end of my bed. She sat there quietly before speaking.

"Ma, what's up? Are you okay?"

She took a deep breath in and exhaled before saying, "I saw him looking at you."

Dom Skinner

I stayed quiet as I waited for her to continue. Her voice deepened as she followed up with, "Did you hear what I said?"

My heart began to race, and my skin boiled. That same rage that I used to feel as a child came back within seconds. I thought that my mind was playing tricks on me. I heard her statement, but her follow-up question felt condemning. As I fought back the tears, I responded, "Yes, I heard you."

Phyllis fired back, "So, that's it? You're not going to say anything about it?"

I could no longer control my voice as I forcefully said, "What would you like me to say? Why are you even talking to me about this? Don't you think this is a conversation you should be having with your boyfriend?"

I could see that she was shocked by my response, but there was no way I could muster up passive aggression. I was so angry that I couldn't hear what she was saying after that. She left my room fussing, but I couldn't hear her words pass the sirens going off in my head. I got out of the bed, closed my bedroom door, and a flood of tears poured out of me. I packed my books and drove to my other home.

The entire drive, I cried and hit the steering wheel.

"God, what did I do to deserve a mother that hates me so much? How is she angry at me?"

~~~

This was the beginning of how our semi-stable relationship ripped into a million pieces until nothing was left. My mother's story started with "I saw him looking at you.", to the worst nightmare, "I know y'all are having an affair."

Within a year, my mother, the woman who birthed me and taught me about morals and integrity, accused me of sleeping

112

with her boyfriend. My world was shattered as she began to treat me like a past friend who had wronged her. Whenever I came to her house, she frowned her face at me before she spoke. I felt the hate. With a broken heart and crushed spirit, I no longer had the tolerance to pretend like I was okay with how she treated me. It was clear that I didn't like my mother. No. Correction. I couldn't stand her, and my words and actions were proof of it.

The wounds deepened every time Phyllis reached out to hug me when others were present. Then, I would feel another cut to my heart when I heard folks praise her for being such a wonderful mother. The slashes felt like the knife was lit on fire before piercing through my flesh. When Phyllis spoke about my accolades and how proud she was, it felt like I was absorbing the flames of a dragon.

I wanted to scream, "Stop lying! You hate me!"

Instead, I thought, "If I yell, I appear childish and weak. Keep your cool. It's not that deep. Your mother hates you, and the feeling is mutual."

During this horrific time, everything seemed unstable. So, I focused on the one thing that always seemed to ground me: school. I focused on my classes and studying for the Graduate Record Examination (GRE) to qualify for graduate school. I figured, "I can't allow this to stop me from being great."

In the process, I lost patience for anything and anyone that seemed like a distraction to my success. Unfortunately, my boyfriend at the time, and his insecurities, were distractions. As a result, I ended the relationship.

As for my mother, Phyllis, I stayed away from her as much as possible. I was no longer serving myself up as her personal punching bag. As far as I was concerned, we had nothing to say to each other. I spoke to her only when absolutely necessary.

Unfortunately, while we were in the thick of our hell, Q wasn't adjusting as well as we'd predicted. Eventually, he moved back to Tarboro. As much as I wanted to support him, I was mentally working overtime to appear put together, and I was struggling at it.

Phyllis and I barely shared words that weren't combative or argumentative throughout my senior year at BSU. I spent most of my days ignoring her phone calls and wishing she'd leave me alone. But my prayers were never answered. Instead, my sisters would call to encourage me to come to dinner or attend an event where our mother would be present. It was an emotional rollercoaster. I felt like no one understood my pain. Not even my parents.

When I spoke about a situation I encountered with Phyllis, they would never join me in my "she's a terrible mother" rant. They'd listen, then tell me how strong I was or how God would take care of it. I didn't want to hear any of that. I wanted them to agree with me. I wanted someone to see my side for once. Yet, instead, I remembered my parents telling Phyllis that they loved her.

"Are you kidding me?"

I was over it. All of it! I guess this was life. I told myself that this was the best I was going to get. So, what did I do? I started to reimagine my life, in my head, until it began to feel real to me. I was already numb to my mother's treatment, so it became easy to suppress my feelings about her. Then, I began to quiet the noise that resembled parental praise. This became my survival technique.

I recognized that Phyllis fed gloriously off compliments from others. Especially when it came to her ability to provide as a mother. Instead of yelling out my truths, I practiced uneasy silence.

Let's Talk

"Phyllis, I love hearing about your girls. Them Skinner girls be doing it, chile. You've done amazing how you raised them girls on your own!" I recall a cousin saying.

So, even though she called me out of my name and tore my character to shreds, she still had to show the world how great she was as a mother. And to show them, it had to all be tangible. Phyllis pulled together resources to pay for my research experience in Ghana, handled all of my graduation fees, and purchased multiple graduation gifts.

"That's my baby and I'm so proud of her. But don't be fooled, she gets it from her mother! She's just like me!", Phyllis would say as she pranced around singing her own praises.

Was I grateful? Sure. Was I annoyed? Absolutely. Was I happy? I had no way of identifying what happiness would look like with my mother, because every moment with her was like walking along a minefield.

I felt like we were at war. While Phyllis was playing nice to be politically correct, and giving the people the mother-daughter dynamic they wanted to love, I was trying to avoid the explosion of one of our slow-burning dynamites. So, when asked to confirm my mother's amazingness, there was always a slightly raised brow and faint chuckle before my response.

"My mother got you everything you wanted. I know you're happy. She loves her some Dominique.", Phyllis' friend uttered.

Trying my best to keep smiling while hoping one of my sisters would call for me, I responded with an underwhelming, "Yep."

Quiet Tears

I graduated from BSU, and I packed up all of my feelings and buried them deep inside me with a "I'm blessed to have adopted parents" sticker on it. Meanwhile, Phyllis was packing up her house and moving to Tarboro, NC in pursuit of her peace. She quit her job and ended her relationship.

Phyllis told everyone who'd listen, "It's time for me to finally have my peace. My youngest child has graduated college and my other daughters are grown and raising their own children. They don't need me anymore." Then, she headed down south. Well, not for long.

Though her furniture was strategically placed in the three-bedroom house that she inherited from her grandmother, and her clothes hung in each of the bedroom closets, she was back in Washington, DC. Phyllis would spend a week or two in Tarboro, then two or three months in DC. Phyllis never had unrestricted time to herself. For as long as she could remember she was responsible for others. Now, Phyllis was discovering how to be responsible for herself, and her actions.

As for me, my graduate program started roughly four weeks after my undergraduate commencement ceremony. Any feelings I had lingering, about my nonexistent relationship with my mother, couldn't stay. I was in the big leagues now, and I didn't have energy to waste. I had to focus on becoming a Clinical Psychologist with a focus in youth development.

My plan was to give back to the community. Honestly, I had no idea what that actually meant. It just sounded good the first time I said it, at my interview for an internship at Morgan Stanley, during my senior year at H.D Woodson. My soon-to-be supervisor was impressed by my statement, and I got the internship. As a result of the positive response I'd received, giving back to the community became part of my elevator pitch.

Being one of the youngest students in my cohort, I felt like the pressure was on for me to prove that I was worthy of my acceptance into the program. Again, I took myself too seriously. No one actually cared about my age or background. Yet, I was spending an extreme amount of energy trying to appear whole and complete. Even perfect, I might add.

"What if I say the wrong thing?

"Just don't say the wrong thing."

"Pull yourself together."

"What if they realize I don't belong here?"

"Don't let them see you sweat."

These thoughts played on repeat as I drove to class during the first week of my program. See, this was my first time out of my comfort zone. Everyone I knew attended high school, except those who found reasons more important outside of school. But they were far and in between. College, yep, same deal. Of course, I knew many folks who'd decided college wasn't for them. But the idea of college was not foreign territory for me.

Except, this was different. I was in graduate school. Not, just graduate school; a clinical psychology program. I know that I said I was going to do it, but I didn't really know anyone who'd taken this route in school. Plus, this program was populated with mostly non-Black students. This was new for me. There were folks from so many different backgrounds and social classes. Who could relate to me, and my crazy story?

I often sat and watched how my new peers interacted with one other. I listened to their choice of discussions unrelated to the clinical field. I felt like an outsider.

Then, I heard my mother's voice. "Lift your head up and sit up straight. Act like you belong in here."

117

"Breath. You got this."

As stated before, no one made me feel like I didn't belong there. Looking back, I can vividly remember feedback from my professors and peers that validated my contribution in our cohort. Yet, I was bringing my unsettled issues with my mother into this new and unfamiliar space. Also, I didn't realize it at the time, but I was slowly reinventing my identity every time someone asked about me or my family.

It was so unnecessary. Except, I still wanted to belong. Two-parent household? Check. Fancy car in the family? Yep, my dad just upgraded my mother's car. Check. Ivy league goer in the family? Dad just completed his master's degree at George Washington University. That's close enough. Check.

The list went on and on. I threw in, "I was adopted.", as an extra layer of truth. But didn't share the full story, so the listeners were left to their own imagination on the details.

The reinvention of my identity wasn't a full lie. But it most definitely was not the full truth. Mainly because I purposely omitted my truths about Phyllis. I'd buried her identity along with the abusive memories. My wounds from her accusations were still fresh. So, I covered it up with a bandage to forget it ever happened.

I spent years in the program wearing different masks that made me feel worthy of the space I was already accepted into. Most days, tears fell from my eyes uncontrollably as I drove from campus to my parents' house. At the time, I wouldn't allow myself to cry in front of others.

"I'm a thug. Tears are for suckers. Pull yourself together."

I would tell myself this as I smiled and interrupted the tears that attempted to make a debut in public. I kept telling myself, "the sharks will eat you alive if you show signs of weakness."

Let's Talk

At the time, I wasn't experiencing sharks or any other dangers. My threats were as real as my reinvented life. There were possible truths, sprinkled with exaggeration. Also, I know real thugs, and I've never participated in activities that would qualify me as a true member. But I gave myself the title as a reminder to toughen up.

Growing up in my house, Phyllis raised us like Helen raised her, and how Celestia brought up Helen. Tears weren't going to solve problems.

"Stop crying before I give you something to cry for."

"Fix your face. Nobody cares about those tears."

These were a few popular sayings in our home. My mother was tough. Unlike me, Phyllis had to be in order to survive. Though I saw her cry, it was never because she felt sorry for herself or her situation. She cried when someone passed away, or while she was praising God throughout the house, or in church. That's it. And she taught us what she knew.

So, I learned the lesson and fixed my face. No, I mastered the lesson, then took it a step further. After a while, I created a persona that informed my mother that I wasn't fazed by how she treated me. I no longer needed to fix my face. It was already done. The mask had been developing since junior high school, and it was now perfect. Flawless, I might add.

It was my favorite mask to wear in graduate school. Any sign of weakness could pierce a hole in my disguise. So, I protected it. I presented myself as the Black, resilient, young woman who was unapologetic about the space I occupied. However, my body would sense privacy when my car door closed, my ignition started, and the seatbelt secured. The moment I would exhale, the mask melted away by the tears and snot that ran down my face.

I'd write in my journal:

Dom Skinner

"I cried again today, but I have no clue why I'm feeling so empty. Maybe I should try to sleep more."

My only logical reason for my uncontrollable tears was my lack of sleep from writing assessment notes. My therapist, at the time, raised her brow as I shared this excerpt from my journal.

She put her pen down and asked, "Do you think your tears have anything to do with your relationship with your biological mother?"

I couldn't believe this was her response, considering I came in to speak about feeling overwhelmed, in school and work. Shifting my body, I responded "No, I doubt that. I typically feel emotional when I don't sleep."

"So, would you say you're emotional most days?", she questioned.

I took a deep breath realizing what just happened. That was checkmate.

"During our first session, you mentioned that you don't sleep much. You said that you spend most of your nights in thought or writing. Are some of the thoughts related to your childhood?", she continued.

How was I in a clinical psychology program and I couldn't figure that out on my own? I guess that is why one of my professors was so adamant about her students being in therapy. "To be an effective therapist, you need to be in therapy.", was her weekly statement.

At that moment, it all made sense. Later in that session, I opened up about some of my more recent interactions with Phyllis.

"Do you think your mother would be open to joining you and your sisters in a family session?", she asked. I laughed so hard. Before I could gather myself to make a sarcastic statement, she continued, "Maybe you should ask her."

It took almost five months before I brought it up to my sisters. Sade' thought it was a great idea. At that point, she was experiencing a rough patch in her relationship with Phyllis and thought therapy could benefit us all. Nekisha was neutral, as always. She didn't mind one way or another. However, she did believe that Sade' and I needed to learn to just let Phyllis be Phyllis.

Nekisha would say, "Y'all know how she is. I don't understand why y'all must go back and forth with her. It's disrespectful. She's your mother, and you only get one mother."

This never sat well with me, so my response was, "I'm not going to allow anyone to lie about me to my face. Not even my mother. The way she treats me like some random chick off the street. That's disrespectful. And even though she gave birth to me, I have another mother."

Ashley, on the other hand, was totally opposed to family therapy. "I don't want to waste my time. She's never going to change.", Ashley stated.

A few days later, we brought it up to Phyllis while sitting in Ashley's living room. Practicing my, newly developed, calm therapeutic voice, I said, "Would you be open to family therapy? I think it'll support us in dealing with some of our issues."

With fireballs, she snapped back, "Issues?!"

I thought, "Damn, I said the wrong word. This isn't going as I planned."

"I don't have issues. There's nothing wrong with me. Something is wrong with y'all. Y'all need help. Maybe they can help y'all figure out why y'all are so disrespectful, after I bend over backwards to give y'all the world." She continued.

121

Ashley interrupted Phyllis' rant with, "I told y'all this was a waste of time."

Eventually, like everyone else, I let it go. I also decided that I was going to protect my peace. I continued to create physical and emotional distance from Phyllis.

Then, before I knew it, I completed my master's degree, the required coursework for my doctoral program, and many clinical practicum hours. I had been on autopilot for so long and needed a break. I was burnt out, tired, empty, and lost.

I knew it was time for me to pause when I was in a team meeting discussing a case, and I became raged about the clinical terms that were being tossed around to describe a client. In my mind, I kept saying, "this person just needs a hug."

The reality was I was that person. I was the one who needed a hug. I'd been disregarding my old and new wounds for the sake of my "well-put-together" proxy, and my perfect stitching started unraveling. It also didn't help that a few weeks prior, the guy that I was dating, at the time, texted me to tell me that he'd just gotten married.

Yep, he had gotten married while I was celebrating Brittany's birthday in Vegas. The night before my flight, he was sharing his love for me. Yet, the morning before my return flight, he was informing me that he'd randomly married another woman. Because I'd been so committed to my "I'm-not-fazed" persona, I said, "Congratulations." I dedicated a few hours to crying, then I blocked his number, fixed my face, boarded my flight, and carried on.

So, as I sat in that meeting, I thought about every child that just needed a hug. My mind went on a journey of its own exploring the debt I was accruing, whether I would be able to afford the next term, and if I was effective in my role as a therapist.

More importantly, I thought, how can I help someone help themselves if I can't help me? The thoughts went on and on. Before I knew it, the meeting was over and the only note I wrote was, "Why am I here?" At that moment, I decided it was time to take a break and turn off the autopilot.

I took the next semester off and stepped into a bigger role at the organization I was working for. I began developing curriculum for youth programs and putting my focus on preventative measures for the communities that the company was serving. This was awesome for me. I didn't have to focus on my issues. More importantly, I could give out those hugs. Similar to the clients that I supported in a professional, or clinical setting, the youth in our programs needed someone to say, "I see you.". I was now that person.

Most of the young people that I'd interacted with were like me. Though they didn't recognize the similarity at first glance because of my wardrobe or the way I spoke, I knew. They weren't just fighting because it was fun. Nor were they just silent because they didn't have anything to say. I was familiar with their patterns, their side-eyes, and nonchalant attitudes. I was even more accustomed to the "come around, but not show too much interest or I won't seem cool" demeanor.

Each one of them was me. Maybe we didn't have the same story or exact path. But there was an emptiness that was present and we all were trying to figure out what it was and how to fill it. I began to pour into them, and into my work that would support them. Then, I took it further. I began coaching track and field at my former junior high school, now called Johnson Middle School. Every opportunity I received to mentor; I took it.

Using my tools as a trained therapist, to love on young people, without labeling them, became my medicine. Some days were difficult, but every interaction was rewarding. To see them smile or witness them peel back a layer of their shell, was like watching a butterfly emerge from its cocoon. I could see the beauty of what's possible for each of them. I guess this is what giving back to the community looked like.

I was putting in countless hours. For the companies I worked for, there were no boundaries. For the students on my track team, there were no boundaries. And for the youth I mentored, no boundaries. Everyone had around-the-clock access to me. They called or texted, no matter the hour, and I answered. I responded. I was present.

Everywhere I turned, I was needed. I felt important. I felt seen. Recognition was everywhere and the accolades came with it. I was even inducted into the Athletic Hall of Fame for track and field at Johnson Middle School. While I didn't know an accomplishment of this magnitude was acknowledged on the middle school level, I was beyond honored. Then, a year later, I became the youngest director in an organization that served the Washington, DC, and Baltimore area.

I guess I was living the dream. But it wasn't dreamy at all. It felt more like a beautiful nightmare. My resume, accomplishments, and influence were a mile long. My work was making an impact. Wasn't this the success I'd pictured? I vividly remember riding in the passenger seat of my father, Vaughn's car, and sharing this life.

"Dad, I just want to be successful."

"What does success look like to you.", my dad asked.

"You know, being in a career where I can make good money and give back to the community."

"Babygirl, follow your passion. Do what makes you happy and the money will come."

I was eighteen years old and had just decided that being a medical doctor was not for me. I was changing my major from biology to psychology. I thought I needed to convince him of my decision. But, after my long perfectly crafted speech, he simply asked, "Are you sure that's what you want to do?"

My father, Vaughn, didn't give me lectures, nor did he try to convince me of anything. He encouraged me to discover answers on my own, trusting that I know what's best for me. My life, my choices. Where everyone else held me to my three-year-old self prophecy of being a doctor, my dad told me daily that he was happy if I was happy. That meant, he didn't care what I decided to do with my life, as long as I was giving it my all.

"Do you want to be average, or do you want to be great?", my dad would ask.

"I want to be great."

"Aight. Well, finish strong. Remember, the mark of a champion is one who never quits."

We've been having this same talk since I was twelve years old, running on his track team. While it started out as a pep talk to get me to run my heart out in the open 400meter sprint, it became the way we communicated about everything. My dad reminded me often that there was nothing I couldn't do, it was just up to whether I was willing to do it. But, as I reminisced on his statement, "do what makes you happy and the money will come.", I couldn't help but get stuck on "makes you happy."

Up until that point, I thought I was doing everything that was supposed to make me happy. I was giving, supporting, and loving. I was even practicing some level of self care. I was exercising, staying hydrated, and seeing a therapist. Well, I would check in with my therapist from time to time. I didn't need to go regularly. I could manage just fine. Or at least that's what I tried to convince myself.

Yet, there were clear signs. No, neon signs that I was, in factor, miserable. There weren't enough awards, titles, accolades, friends, passport stamps, outfits, or beaming smiles to persuade my inner child that she had made it to the other side. Instead, my perfect stitching that I'd been crafting over the decades was steadily unraveling.

While I was trying to be the savior in everyone's life, I didn't realize that I was the one who needed rescuing. It looked like the medicine was either wearing off or it was just a placebo. Something needed to be done. I had to figure out what was killing me on the inside.

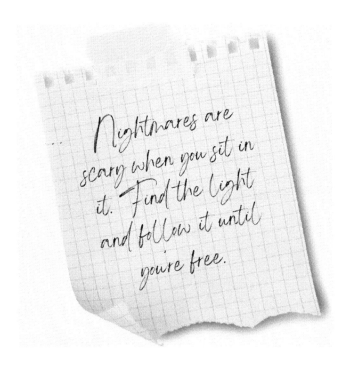

Chapter Seven:

I See You

Dom Skinner

For years, my best friend, Brittany, had been expressing her concerns about my superhero complex. Brittany and I have been friends since we were 14 years old, and she had the front-row seat and backstage pass to the show of my life. When I needed to slow down, she didn't have a problem bringing me back to reality.

Brittany is the polar opposite of me. She's reserved and quiet. But when she speaks, she's a straight shooter. She doesn't beat around the bush or make nonsense sound pretty. She's my voice of reason.

Over the years, she'd been offering me the same advice. "You know that you can say no." I would spend hours telling her about the million and one things I had on my to-do list, then finish up by talking about how tired I was. Brittany would say, "say no and go to sleep. It's not that difficult."

Every time Brittany offered her wise words, I'd pile on all the reasons why I had to be the one to complete the tasks, or what could happen if I didn't do it. Brittany isn't going to argue with anyone. It's just not her style. If "I said what I said" was a person, it would be Brittany Robinson. So, when I followed up with my statements like I was a defense attorney, Brittany would respond, "Well, do you boo."

However, friends like Brittany, don't sit back and watch you suffer. No matter how good I was at convincing the world, and myself, that I was fine, Brittany saw through my disguise.

Since Brittany and I didn't encounter issues as roommates during our freshman year at Winston-Salem State, we decided it would be cool to live together again, years later, as adults. One night, as I sat at our shared dining room table, typing up a report at 12:30am, and scratching the hives that were forming on the back of my hands and arms, Brittany stood across from me and said, "You've got to stop this."

"I'm almost done. I just need to finish the last point.", I responded.

"No, you don't. They can wait. The world isn't going to end if you don't finish the report right now."

"I know it won't. I just have a lot to do tomorrow, and I need to get this out of the way." I said as I paused from typing to scratch some more.

Then, the light from my cell phone grabbed my attention. It was a message from one of my colleagues from work. But, before I could read the full message, Brittany snatched my phone from my hand.

"Dominique, stop it. Look at you. You are literally breaking out in hives because of the stress from this job."

"Naw, I think it's something I ate. Brit, I promise I'll stop working in 30 minutes. Let me just check the message. I don't want to miss anything for tomorrow."

Tears started forming in her eyes as she calmed her voice. "This is not healthy, friend. You are killing yourself for a job that you hate. This is not okay. You need to rest. Go to sleep."

"I don't know how.", I said as tears started to pour out of me. "I'm exhausted, but I can't sleep. My mind won't slow down."

Brittany gently closed my laptop and told me to breathe. As I sat there crying uncontrollably, Brittany disappeared into my bathroom. When she returned, she informed me that she had started a bath for me, she lit the candles in my bedroom, and that she would make me some hot tea. She then instructed me to go get in the tub.

So, I did. By the time I returned to my room, my space was filled with the calming aroma of lavender and the sounds of gently crashing waves were coming through my speaker. After about 30 minutes of deep breathing, I melted away in a deep sleep.

I wish I could say that I was forever changed after that moment; that I realized the hives were from stress, or that I began creating boundaries. The truth is nothing had changed. My behavior and excuses remained the same. I still hadn't learned the magic of saying "No". Well not entirely, I said "No" more than I said "Yes" to my mother, Phyllis.

When she called, I'd see "Ms. Skinner" pop up on my screen, and say, "Nope. I'm not dealing with that today."

Then, I would press decline to send her straight to voicemail. Just seeing her name on my phone screen was enough to flare up something in my spirit. My mood would change as I went down a list of reasons why she would call me. I would become frustrated and annoyed for hours.

Whenever Phyllis asked to ride with me to an event, I was quick to respond. "Nope, I won't be staying long, and have other places to go after.". I found every excuse possible to keep physical and mental distance from my mother. If I couldn't muster up the decency to answer most of her phone calls, I didn't think I was free enough to willingly ride in the car with her.

Other than that, I was everyone's "I got you" girl. Yet, after a while, I felt worn out and realized Brittany was right. I did hate my job and was exhausted from playing superhero. Don't get me wrong, I enjoyed making an impact in the lives of others. But I wasn't fulfilled. I was back on autopilot, doing what I thought I was supposed to do. In my mind, this was another version of the big leagues; the titles and being in big rooms that seemed important with people who thought I was important. But what was I doing here?

I remembered a conference that I attended for work. I sat next to an older gentleman during lunch who'd asked me about my journey. During my share, I stated that I was going back to school to finish up my doctorate degree. When he asked why, I told him because I was so close to finishing. He shared that he'd earned his Ph.D. in theater yet spent most of his career in the environmental field. Before we returned to the breakout rooms, he said to me, "Time is something you can't get back. Don't waste it."

I was twenty-eight years old, and I was doing everything but nothing that fulfilled me. I was giving away time and there was no way I could get it back. But how was I supposed to save it? Or savor it?

I was confused but didn't have the time to research it. I was preparing my track team for a championship. They needed a win. We needed a win. If I couldn't get back this time, I was going to make sure those kids knew I fought for them and with me.

Then, there was Brittany, back in her same position, looking at me with her hand on her hip and head slightly tilted to the side. "Okay, I've been thinking. You should really be acting. You're wasting your talent."

"What talent?", I thought, as I continued adding names to my relay chart.

"Bee, I don't have time for this right now. I'm trying to put together this championship schedule.", I said annoyed.

"You said that you wanted to be more spontaneous and that you were going to be more creative."

"But I wasn't talking about acting."

"But, why not. That can be you on the TV.", as she pointed towards our living room television.

"Girl, I don't know the first thing about acting." I said, dismissing her.

Brittany had been saying, "You should be an actress." since the day I met her. And throughout the years, whenever I get comfortable enough to go "full in" as I tell a story, she reminded me. But it was something about the way she was saying it this time. She was serious.

Earlier that year, she and I were walking around Adams Morgan after having bottomless mimosas at brunch. While in a random shop, we came across a few guys who were on a road trip from Miami to New York. They were actors and musicians. Up until that point, we'd never met screen actors before. I thought they were joking, so when they asked if I was an actress, I looked at them seriously and said, "Naw, I'm a drug dealer." I don't know why that was the first thing that came to my mind, but I said it.

These guys were different from those we knew and experienced in DC. They were funny and free. They had spontaneity written all over them. Brittany and I, who were both overly calculated individuals, wanted what they had. I exchanged numbers with one of the guys to stay in contact.

A few weeks later, Brittany and I were still talking about their spirits, so we tried on the spontaneity hat to see how it fit us. We booked our flights for that weekend to Miami, then told them we were coming to visit. It was awesome. It just so happened that one of them just got their show picked up by a network and was in pre-production while we were visiting. I decided to travel back down to Miami a few weeks later and was able to see the magic in action. I spent a few hours on set just witnessing the beautiful world of make-believe.

It was amazing. It was lively, I can admit. But, at that moment, I was not thinking about stepping away from my comfortable lifestyle that allowed me to receive a salary every two weeks. But all Brittany could think about was, "that's what Dom is supposed to be doing."

133

As I sat at the dining room table scheduling out the championship lineup, Brittany's next question was the push that created a pivot on my path.

"If I pay for your first acting class, would you go?"

"Well, hell yea, I'd go, if you're paying." I said, thinking that she was joking.

She sat down, across from me, and turned my laptop to face her. Then, began searching acting courses in the Washington, DC area.

"Oh, she's serious?", I thought. And she was as serious as a heart attack.

The following month, I was walking in the doors of The Theater Lab, in Washington, DC. This entry-level course was simply that, an introduction. And it was EVERYTHING! I played and imagined, and played some more, for three hours. I felt free!

"This is a great outlet from work," I thought. "I'm going to do this again."

After a few months, I was tossing and turning while trying to get my mind to stop roaming. It was 3am and I'd been up since the day before. I was exhausted, and my 6am CrossFit class was hours away.

"Why am I still up?" I said aloud as I sat up in my bed.

I grabbed my journal from my nightstand and started writing out my thoughts, so I could free up some mental space to sleep. Before I knew it, the sun was coming up and I'd written pages about living versus existing. The last few sentences I wrote before closing the journal, and my eyes, were:

~~~

"If I only get this one life to live, or if I can only experience one life at a time, I don't want to just exist. I want to LIVE. I want to live fully. God, Brittany has been saying that I should act since I've known her, but if you're giving me a message through her, make it clear. Let me know it's real."

~~~

The next day, I began speaking it. I'm going to pursue acting. Like being three years old and saying I was going to be a doctor, I had no clue how it was going to happen. But I said it. Then, a few people that I had spoken to about it said I should talk to this person and that person. Before I knew it, I had information that I didn't know existed. My large network was growing larger.

I began auditioning and taking more classes, even improv. I was on a new path, and I was trusting the journey. Almost magically, I began feeling lighter, like a weight was lifted off my shoulders. It was extremely interesting considering I hadn't quit my job, I was still coaching track, I was still in a romantic relationship that wasn't good for me, and it was still shaky territory with my mother. While nothing in my life had changed, I was feeling different, in the best way.

"Is this what life is like when I ask God to reveal something to me?", I thought. "Maybe, I should do this with everything else."

The only thing stopping us from clarity is our belief that it doesn't exist.

The Talk

In my very plush position as a director, I enjoyed the luxury of working from home, at a coffee shop, on the road, or wherever. Honestly, it was the only perk of my job considering I was often working around the clock. Everyone in my life knew I didn't have a traditional work schedule, so I would get calls for all kinds of mid-day requests; take someone to the airport, pick someone up from school, etc.

I was responsible enough to let folks know that I actually have a job. But the one person who made the most outrageous requests was my mother, Phyllis. She didn't care how many times I told her no, or reminded her that I had responsibilities at my job. Phyllis would still make her requests.

It had been years since she'd accused me of having a sexual affair with her ex-boyfriend. But the wounds felt fresh. While it was less about the past accusations, the pain felt like new attacks every time she pretended that we were the best of buddies in the company of others, or when she questioned my coldness towards her.

"I don't know what I did to hurt you so much that you can't stand to hear my voice." She'd scoff. "If I did anything to hurt you, I'm sorry."

"If", I thought to myself. I'd just remain quiet, as I exhale loudly, roll my eyes, and walk away.

She'd get louder as her voice would crack while she tried to hold back tears that would eventually stream down her face.

"I don't know why God gave me such disrespectful daughters. Y'all won't appreciate me until I'm dead and gone. Every day I wish my mother was still here. I'm alive and you won't even acknowledge me as your mother."

Let's Talk

"This is exactly why I stay away." I would say under my breath as I head to my car, or another room if I was forced to stay at the location.

Like in my teenage years, I was undoubtedly passive-aggressive towards my mother. And the coldness she felt between us was my protective shield over my wounded heart. It was hard to see her as my mother after being treated like a random woman that she despised. Though she ended her relationship with her ex-boyfriend, changed her address, and maybe found that peace she was searching for, but I was still wounded, and forgiveness was just the words I uttered.

So, when I received requests from Phyllis, my first thought was always, "No!" More than likely, one of my sisters would call on her behalf and I would change my mind. But if I did, I didn't complete the request with a smile or joy. I was pissed. I would huff and puff the entire time. This was my exact behavior when Phyllis asked me to drive her to Tarboro, and then back to DC, just for her to sign some papers.

We are in the age of technology where electronic signatures are a thing. Yet, if we must take it a step back, a print, sign with a pen, scan the document, then email it would work too. I didn't understand the logic of me driving, in the car with my mother, for hours, by myself, on a Wednesday. Plus, I had work to do.

"Ma, you do know I work, right?", I said. "Plus, I have a meeting tomorrow. Why can't you drive yourself?"

"Yea, I know you work. My car is in the shop, and I have to sign those papers for my house. I need to meet with them in person. It's just a quick drive there and back. We can leave at 4 am and be back before 3pm. I'll drive so you can do your work."

She had it all figured out. But I didn't care. I still said it wasn't going to work for me. Seconds after hanging up from our call. Something in my spirit said, "go." It was weird. I was good at convincing myself that I made the right choice.

There was no way I wanted to spend almost 12 hours with my mother, without one of my sisters there as a buffer. I didn't want to experience the heavy and awkward energy. It was too much. But my spirit wasn't allowing me to feel good about my decision.

A few minutes later, I called back. "Ma, I'll take you. Please be ready at 4am. I have to be back no later than 4pm to get ready for my 5pm meeting."

"Really? Aww, thank you, baby girl. I really appreciate this. I will fill your car up for you. And maybe while we're there you can see…"

I cut her off, "We're not going to see anybody. You're signing your papers and we're getting back on the road. Okay?"

"Okay! I just thought since you haven't been to Tarboro in a while, you'd like to see…"

"Alright, ma." I said cutting her off again. "I have to get going. I have to finish up some stuff before my next call."

"Well, aight then. I'll see you in the morning. Dominique, I really appreciate this. I love you.", she said softly.

"Yea, no worries. Bye"

As I drove to Delvon's house to pick up Phyllis, I had to talk to God. I told God to give me strength to get through this trip. I let Him know that I had no idea why my spirit told me to agree, but it must have been Him. So, if He was trying to reveal something to me, He needed to make it clear.

Oh, did God make it clear. After a few uncomfortable statements and accusations about how I feel about her, why I treat her like a stranger, etc., I calmed my voice and I just breathed. Eventually, I shared about my secret depressive episodes, the anxiety that I've experienced since I was a child, and how I'd been in and out of therapy for years because of it. Most importantly, I shared that most of it developed out of my relationship with her.

Phyllis is Phyllis and she had her moments where she took the opportunity to talk about herself. She recalled her childhood with her mother and how she worked to be different. These were stories I'd heard before, and it almost felt like an excuse, which made me feel like she was dismissing my words. But then something changed. She wanted to hear more from me.

She began asking me questions. In the calmest voice, I opened up; I shared that I do appreciate all that she had given me AND many events from my childhood caused our current relationship to be what it is. I poured out the details of every event, or situation, I could remember since I was five years old and what I felt in those moments. More importantly, I revealed that I never felt loved, or seen, by her.

Through sobbing tears, my mother put her hands on mine and said, "I'm so sorry."

The tension from my body was released. I'd never heard this in her voice. I turned to meet her eyes and I knew she meant every word.

"I'm sorry for all of the pain I've caused you. I love you so much. You are my baby girl. I thank God every day for you. I was trying my best. I didn't think you would remember some of the things I said. I was hurting. I was frustrated. I was tired. I said things because I was angry, but it had nothing to do with you or your sisters. I wish I could take it back."

"Ma, we can't go back in the past. But we can move forward. I didn't know it, but I guess all I ever wanted was for you to say, 'I'm sorry' and for you to see me".

"Please know that I really am sorry for all of it. Even with everything that happened with that old man of mine. I was in a dark place. You're my baby, and I raised you. I know you're not that type of person. I wish we had a better relationship."

"We may never have the relationship your friends have with their daughters, but we can start from somewhere. I'd like to get to know you and I think you might like getting to know me as well."

That day, on that drive, it was God, my mother, and me. It was raw, it was vulnerable, and it was us. No masks, no preconceived notions, and no weapons. We both let go and decided to see each other, the good, the bad, and the ugly.

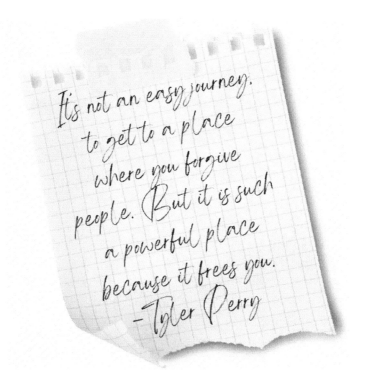

It's not an easy journey,
to get to a place
where you forgive
people. But it is such
a powerful place
because it frees you.
— Tyler Perry

Chapter Eight:

We Get to Heal

Dom Skinner

After that drive with my mother, Phyllis, my eyes began to open more. God was really talking to me. That spirit that was pushing me to say yes to spending a day driving to and from Tarboro was God. The drive had nothing to do with the papers my mother needed to sign. Yet, it had everything to do with the air that needed clearing.

I began to think, "what else do I need to clear out?"

A few weeks later, I took a drive to South Carolina to attend a random talent search audition. It was one of those opportunities that targeted new aspiring actors. They asked you to pay thousands of dollars to audition in front of agents and managers, and possibly have an opportunity to sign with a company on the spot. It's super sketchy. But I wasn't aware, and I was beyond naïve. So, I gave my hard-earned money to that company and drove down i95 highway to that audition.

Phyllis asked if I could drop her off in Tarboro since it was in the same direction. I agreed. This drive was different. We talked a little more than usual, but it wasn't smooth. We had our moments of being uncomfortable, like a couple trying to figure out life together after one of them cheated. Overall, it wasn't terrible. However, it was informative. It became obvious that I was actively hurting my mother with my sarcasm and my nonchalant demeanor. If I'm honest, I was in a dark place and I was taking my frustration out on her.

This is what they mean when they say, "Hurt people, hurt people." This is what happened with my mother, and why she was throwing daggers at me and my sisters. She hadn't dealt with her mess, so she was taking it out on who was around her. Now, I was experiencing the same thing.

I'd been in and out of a relationship with the same person who'd gotten married to someone else while we were dating. A year or so after he'd gotten married, he and his wife had separated. After the countless calls, letters, and messages explaining his side of the story and apologizing, I finally accepted his call. I slowly took my walls down and let him back into my life. He wanted me. No, he expressed it as needing me. And who doesn't want to be wanted? Plus, I was still desperate for love.

Yet, over the years, I'd break up with him because I didn't believe that he valued me. Months would pass and he'd return, pledging his love for me and why he needed me in his life. He would spell out all the reasons why he loved me. Time after time, I'd get back on the ride knowing that I shouldn't. But I was in love with the idea of being in love, at the same time, battling with worthiness.

While driving to South Carolina, after dropping Phyllis off in Tarboro, I turned the music off, and I began speaking out loud to God. I released every bit of control. Tears ran down my face as I screamed to let it all out. I was losing my mind. I was so low. I felt empty and I could no longer hide it. My mother said she was sorry, and I could see that she was trying, but I was still a mess. What was it?

~~

"God, I'm letting go. I can't do this anymore. I've been trying for so long, and I'm exhausted. This can't be it for me. Why am I here? Why did you create me? Please let me know. Tell me what to do. Do you want me to leave my relationship? -- Wait, what? Why would I say that? -- God, is that what you want me to do? If so, I'll do it if you want me to. I just need strength because I don't have it on my own. Do you want me to be acting? I don't know what I'm doing. Tell me where to go. Send me who I need. Guide me. I want to live, so I'm surrendering my life to you."

~~

Every day since that dramatic cry and speech to God, I've practiced quieting the noise I've created in my mind to follow God's direction. Two weeks later, I ended my relationship and closed that door forever. That night, after I cried tears of relief, I slept for 13 hours. When I woke up, I didn't have to pretend I was okay. I honestly felt great.

A month later, Brittany and I started a podcast. "Okay, creativity!", I thought.

I believed this was it, and my purpose was being revealed. Then, God told me to move to LA. I knew that I needed to leave DC to step away from my comfort zone, especially if I was going to really pursue acting. Something in my heart told me that I wouldn't go full in if I stayed at home.

While my sight was not set on the west coast, I'd made a promise to surrender. So, I trusted the vision that I'd received in my meditation and made a plan. Like everything else, I shared my vision and it started manifesting before my eyes.

In May of 2019, I left my career and moved across the country to Los Angeles, California. The following month, I started my intensive acting training in an acting conservatory program, at the American Musical and Dramatic Academy (or AMDA). The unfolding was breathtaking, and I wouldn't have believed it if it wasn't happening in real time.

During my first year in LA, I went through a journey that opened my eyes wider. Being in an uncomfortable space was humbling to me. I was no longer covered with my accolades or titles. Nor did I have the comforts of a salary, which every artist knows can come with its own set of challenges.

Yet, it was new. It was bare. And, it was calm. But, more than anything, it was uncomfortably comfortable. This was the first time, in a long time, that I wasn't sure, or had a plan. Other than training, developing a network, and telling stories, I didn't have a clear outline for the journey. Honestly, I still don't.

My plan is to be present so I can enjoy living every moment. When I told God that I was going to follow wherever He led me, I meant it. I trusted that God would begin creating my path and my new career. And it's true, and currently happening. However, I had no clue that God was going to evolve me.

Through my daily prayers and meditations, my walls started to fall, my masks began to burn, and my wounds started healing. My heart has found a new posture. It's been opened to receive a new story.

Consequently, my relationship with my biological father, Checko, is healthy and beautiful. We never spoke about the past. But we speak quite a lot about everything that feeds our relationship. Through our new connection, I've discovered that we have the same laugh. I'm also learning that he has a lot of wisdom to share, and I'm soaking up all of it.

Additionally, I have a new appreciation for my godfather, Steve. I now understand what he meant when he said that I was too young to understand. While I thought I wasn't enough, his actions told a different story. And that's the story I'm holding in my heart.

Since taking the leap of faith and uprooting my life in DC, people from all journeys found their way to my path, and I discovered love in a new way. I was constantly asked to serve by helping my new friends communicate their feelings to their peers, to listen and see a different perspective of their parents, or simply reminding them that they are worthy of occupying space in exactly who they are.

I began to believe that my voyage with Phyllis was so I could support others as they journey through what they saw as misfortunes. I found myself speaking about my mother's sacrifices as I described why I appear so protective of those I love. When I cooked a meal and shared my dinner table with friends, I told stories about how Phyllis made sure we were in the kitchen while she cooked, so we could learn.

Let's Talk

As I cried with a friend and told her to lift her head up and remember that she belonged in the room, I felt Phyllis' voice come out of my mouth. When someone was in need and I offered my couch as a safe place for them to reset, I trusted my mother's words, "God blessed you, so don't be afraid to bless others."

Though I live across the country from my mother, her essence is still near. Her words find their way through me. Her lessons are the evidence of how I live my life. So, I no longer pretend to have a perfect childhood story. My story is a beautiful mess.

I no longer hide my mother's existence. I share that I was adopted out of pure love, and yes, I know my biological mother, because she raised me. My family is large and blended. It's fun to say I have a gang of parents and I am everywhere in the birth order. I'm Phyllis' youngest, Checko's middle, and the Perry's oldest.

It's true, Phyllis still gets on my last nerve. She is loud, opinionated, and unapologetic about it all. She is also sweet, giving, and so much fun. She is my mother, and I am my mother's daughter. I am part of her and so much more because she created a path for me to be so.

My mother isn't just a mother. She is human. Before she gave birth to her first child, she was a child. Then, she became a mother and had to figure it out. She didn't get a magical handbook that spelled out the rules of parenting, because it doesn't exist. But, even if she did, how can you follow along when the variables keep changing? Yet, without a superhero cape, she did the best she could with what she had. Where my mother fell short, God added in the missing pieces.

After riding along a crazy roller coaster with my mother, I realized that I always had the choice to get off. The world is filled with choices. Like my mother, I do not have to accept my circumstances. So, I'm no longer accepting the narrative that my mother did not love me. I'm changing it.

My mother loves me in her love language. While she didn't know how to be vulnerable enough to hug me in my youth, I'm accepting every one of her hugs now. Our relationship isn't perfect, but we're finding our way. Together, we now understand that words are molds that can shape good and bad, no matter the intention. Since we know that words mean things, we never end a call without saying, "I love you."

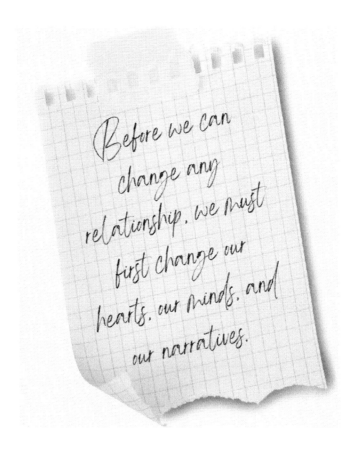

> You may have to crawl before you can walk, but it's time for you to start moving again.

SARAH JAKES ROBERTS

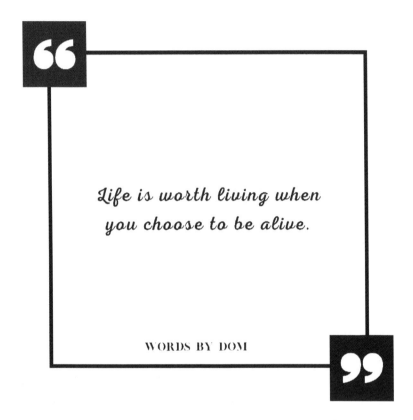

Life is worth living when
you choose to be alive.

WORDS BY DOM

Acknowledgments

My heart is so full! I wrote a book! I wrote this book for you. I see you and you are more than enough. As Heather L. Lawrence would say, "You are worthy simply because you exist."

This book could not have been possible without the journey I've traveled with my beautiful mother, Phyllis Skinner. Mommy, thank you for sharing your stories with us during our long summer road trips. All you wanted was for my sisters and me to understand your life, so we'd appreciate your sacrifices. I see you. I appreciate you. More importantly, I finally get it. You are one of a kind, and I love you!

In addition to my mother, I'd like to acknowledge my ride-or-die gang, my sisters, Nekisha, Ashley, and Sade', and brother Delvon Bullock. Together, there is nothing we can't do! Thank you for paving the way for me to be great. Thank you for protecting me, supporting me, and holding me to my highest potential. Of course, my sibling list isn't complete. I can't miss the opportunity to say "I love you" to the rest: Steve Douglas, Alyssa Douglas, Stacy Jones, Tia Jones, Shantal Jones, Neka Jones, Johari Stewart-Perry, Zander Perry, and Rylee Mae Perry. You got me, and I got you. It's a forever thing.

To the rest of my family, thank you for being my biggest cheerleaders. A special thank you to my aunt, Christine, my uncles, Nathaniel and Brian, and to my cousins, Marcus, and Beverly for pushing me to stay true to myself and my visions.

Furthermore, I would have never taken the first step into storyteller without the 14-year push from my best friend, Brittany Robinson. Thank you, friend, for being my voice of reason.

To the entire Momentum Education family, this is just the floor. I don't know what I don't know, but I've found my awareness. I am on my skinny branch while I choose to live my dream now. Thank you for an invitation to play to win.

Lastly, thank you to my buddies, my team. I am forever grateful for every moment and resource you've invested into this journey. When each of you said, "I got you!" I felt it. Jessica Alexandra Cancino, Nancy Aragbaye, Lavarro Jones, Kyara Butler, Jackqueline Lou, James "Jimmy" Watkins, Ciara Talley, Shanice McDonald, Kaien Cruz, Giulianna Pino, Monique Cook, Sarneshea Evans, Genora Givens, Ale' Romero, Jolisa Brooks, Mo Brown Suga, and, Yannick Eike Mirko.

About the Author

Dom Skinner is an actress, writer, storyteller, mentor, and educator. She is also a daughter, a niece, and an auntie. Dom has become an ambassador of love and healing through changing the narrative of our stories.

Dom was born and raised in Washington, DC, and had every intention to save lives as a doctor. Her path changed courses and sent her down the road of clinical psychology, where she spent years in youth development and mentorship.

When she decided to leave her comfort zone to follow her visions, Dom started her acting journey in Los Angeles, CA. There she began healing from her childhood. Through her healing, Dom began to live in her worthiness. Now, she has every intention to save lives through her stories.

Made in the USA
Las Vegas, NV
06 November 2023

80352515R00090